YOUTH MINISTRY L
turning "sour" experiences intc

YOUTH MINISTRY
LEMONADE

*Turning "Sour" Experiences into
Leadership Success*

*Jay Abiera • Paul Armitage • Andrew Bonaventura
Joshua Becker • John Byrne • Peter Doan
Andy Geffers • Matt Genos • Joel Lusz
Kent Julian • Steven Julian*

dedication

This book is dedicated to the incredible youth ministry volunteers that each of the contributing authors has had the privilege to serve alongside. Our lives are richer because of you! You've helped us learn valuable leadership lessons, especially as we've struggled through our "sour" experiences, and together we have discovered how to make Youth Ministry Lemonade. Thanks for pressing on—your commitment to serving Christ by loving teenagers inspires us!

Contents

Introduction: A Bowl of Lemons — Kent Julian   9

Lemon 1: Hitting the Basics; Missing the Basis
    (Overlooking the Main Thing) — Joshua Becker   13

Lemon 2: Atomic Elbows and Montana Nights
(It's So Much More Than Hype) — Steven Julian   23

Lemon 3: God, Are You Sure You Want Me?
    (Being the Leader God Created You to Be) — Andy Geffers   35

Lemon 4: I Got This!
    (Leaving God Out of the Success Equation) — Jay Abiera   47

**Lemon 5: From Plexi-Glass to Tube Socks . . . And I'm
Not Talking Indoor Soccer**
    (Restoring Credibility after Offending Others) — Paul Armitage   57

Lemon 6: When Innovations Don't Get Standing Ovations
    (Making Changes the Wrong Way)
    — Andrew Bonaventura   69

Lemon 7: If I Had Only Been Known
    (Leading Through Biblical Community) — John Byrne   79

Lemon 8: Radar Detector on the Dashboard of Life

    (Detecting Trials and Learning from Them) — Peter Doan   89

Lemon 9: From Aliens to Allies

    (Partnering with Parents) — Joel Lusz   99

Lemon 10: When Your Circle of Trust Implodes

    (Knowing Who, When, and How to Trust Others) — Matt Genos   109

Conclusion: Mixing Youth Ministry Lemonade

    (Final Thoughts to Sweeten Your Leadership) — Kent Julian   121

introduction

a bowl of lemons

by Kent Julian

*Mistakes are like stop signs . . . a signal that it's time to learn something new,
something you did not know before.*[1]

- Robert Kiyosaki -

Have you ever said: "If I could just do one thing over again. . . . ?"
I have!

More often than I like to admit.

In middle school, I made a huge mistake. No need for details; let's
just say that for a seventh grader, the mistake and circumstances were
colossal. After the dust settled, I often thought, "If I could just live that
moment over again. . . ."

Or how about in my early 20's when I was engaged to a wonderful
young woman? As we moved closer to the wedding date, we realized
something was wrong. No "major issues," we just started recognizing
that marriage wasn't right for us. We were confused, disoriented, and
once the wedding was off . . . devastated. For months afterwards I said to
myself, "If only I could go back and make changes, neither of us would
be hurting so much."

There was even that time in ministry when I served in a church for only nine months. Ouch, this one really hurt! After having a track record of "success" in two other ministries, I moved to a new church with great anticipation, only to leave when the school year ended. To this day I still haven't figure out exactly what happened. The church was great—back then and today. It's impacting its community and the world. The lead pastor is a man for whom I have much respect. So why wasn't it a good fit for me? What did I miss? How could I have uprooted my family, moved to another state, and then do it all over again nine months later?

pushing different buttons

If my life were a bowl of fruit, there would be many lemons in it. Not just lemons; there would be lip-smacking pieces of fruit like strawberries of success, apples of achievement, and mangos of joy. Yet there would still be those lemons! Mistakes, missteps, mess-ups, and misfortunes. Most not too bitter; but some downright sour.

For years, I've tried to figure out ways to avoid lemons. Dodging, ducking, erasing, and evading. Yet no matter how hard I try, lemons just seem to be a part of my life.

And therein lays one of the most basic facts of life: *life is full of lemons.*

Now I'm not stupid . . . I knew lemons are a part of life; but like many people, it hadn't sunk into my heart. Deep down inside, I felt like I could somehow, someway, avoid lemons. Yet after my most difficult-to-understand sour experience (the nine month tenure at the church mentioned above), I was challenged by two men to push different buttons. Here's basically what they said:

> *Pushing the "why" and "if only" replay buttons over and over again is the wrong approach. Either button takes you down the wrong path. In fact, you will never accomplish anything as a leader without experiencing failure. What's more, most failures usually hold keys to success, because within failure are the hidden lessons of life. Failures cause people to be changed at the core of their beings and allow them to lead*

with authenticity, credibility, and character. So in some ways, you actually want to fail. It's not that you want to go out of your way to fail; but when it happens, embrace it, learn from it, and then move on.

These words were an AH-HA experience for my heart! I stopped pushing the "why" and "if only" replay buttons, and started pushing "what's the lesson" and "where do I go from here" buttons.

youth ministry lemonade

This book is all about helping you experience the same kind of AH-HA moment I experienced, so that your "sour" youth ministry missteps can lead to leadership successes. Ten youth workers just like you share major mistakes from their ministries and examine how God, in his grace, used these events to teach them valuable lead-

> Since my AH-HA experience, I have devoured books about turning failure into success. Some of my favorites have been: *The Making of a Leader* by Robert Clinton, *Failing Forward* by John Maxwell, *Overcoming the Dark Side of Leadership* by Gary McIntosh and Samuel Rima, and *The Top Ten Mistakes Leaders Make* by Hans Finzel. Other books that are not necessarily about turning failure into success, but do have significant insight on the subject include *Pour Your Heart Into It* by Howard Schultz, *QBQ* by John Miller, and *Before You Quit Your Job* by Robert Kiyosaki.

ership lessons. The stories are real. Some are humorous, a few are serious, and most are intense. But bottom line, they are real life scenarios that you will likely face. Our hope is that these stories will save you from making the same mistakes we've made. And while what my two friends said was true—learn from your failures and move on—an even wiser approach is this: *learn from other people's mistakes and you'll save yourself some time and pain.* And that's why we wrote this book.

So together, let's mix some youth ministry lemonade.

Joshua Becker

Joshua Becker began ministering to students over eight years ago as a youth ministry volunteer. Since 1998, he has served youth ministries in Nebraska, Wisconsin, and Vermont. Currently, he serves as the Pastor of Student Ministries at Essex Alliance Church in Essex Junction, Vermont, where he oversees a ministry of 250+ students. Joshua has become a frequent speaker at youth ministry events, camps, retreats, and training seminars. He received a Bachelor's degree in Banking and Finance from the University of Nebraska and a Master's degree of Theological Studies from Bethel Seminary.

Joshua has been married to his wife, Kim, for seven years. In his free time, he enjoys playing ball with his son, Salem, and spending quality time with his daughter, Alexa. He also enjoys sports, reading, a beautiful New England summer evening, and a good bleu cheese salad dressing.

To contact Joshua:
becker@essexalliance.org
802.878.8213

hitting the basics; missing the basis

(overlooking the MAIN thing)

Love is a fruit in season at all times, and within reach of every hand.

—Mother Teresa

Before we go any further, I'd like you to do something. Close your eyes for a couple of minutes and answer this question: In what real ways has God shown that He loves you during the past week?

I started our Wednesday night meeting a little bit differently that week. I followed the short 3-4 minute spiritual exercise listed above with a teaching about God's love from I John. It had been an intense week of God working in my life, and I remember being nervous wondering if my lesson was going to connect with students as deeply as it connected with me. It did. Far from being typical, that night proved to be a major turning point in my ministry.

four years of frustration

I walked into my first full-time youth ministry position six years ago in typical youth pastor fashion. I had a college education. I had good communication skills. I had good looks; at least, my wife thought so. I had confidence; probably too much. I had an active prayer life. I had good training after completing a two year internship. I knew how to do youth ministry, so that is what I did.

I did everything that I knew how to do. And I must say, I did it well. I made Sunday morning an exciting place to be with snacks, games, and good teaching. I established a strategic small group ministry on Wednesday nights and planned the biggest Friday night outreach events that my budget could afford. I launched a ministry team to "equip the saints." I worked hard following the youth ministry model that I had been taught.

After the first two years, however, it became clear that my ministry was not becoming all that I knew it could become. Our attendance was sluggish at best. Students did not seem to have a passion for Christ and the number of lost students who had accepted Christ could be counted on one hand. I could not understand why. I thought I was doing everything that a youth ministry does: Bible studies, outreach events, ministry teams, contacting students, retreats, summer trips, excellence, etc. I was doing it all. But I knew something had to change.

I began looking for a new system and strategy. I read the latest youth ministry books and journals. I attended the biggest conferences. I changed our program to match the newest youth ministry growth strategies. I became more creative in my communication. We began meeting on different nights. Still, nothing substantial changed in the hearts of my students. Passion for Christ was still not growing. I knew something was missing, but had no idea what. Little did I know the very thing I was missing just happened to be one of the most important truths in all of Scripture and the cornerstone of Jesus' ministry.

a week that changed my life forever

Then came a week so influential in my life I still remember it vividly years later. In one week, I read the writings of three different men who wove together a truth so obvious I couldn't believe I had missed it for so many years. Gary Thomas, in his book *Seeking the Face of God*, showed me that seeking holiness for holiness sake is actually idolatry, and that the true essence of holiness is loving God. Through Will Walker's blog, *Musings*, I learned that only with true love for God will our deepest desires and sinful tendencies begin to change. The Apostle John in his letter, *1 John*, showed me that only when we begin to comprehend and experience God's love for us will we begin to love him in response.

The spiritual truth that changed my life forever came into focus: *Only after people begin to truly fathom God's love for them will their lives begin to change on the inside and the outside.*

That was the week I realized what I had been missing. I had made the mistake of neglecting to communicate God's love. For four long wheel-spinning years, my ministry had become a place where I taught students *how* to follow Jesus Christ but had never communicated the reason *why* to follow Jesus Christ. I had been urging students over and over again to give their lives completely over to God but had never systematically presented this God, with my words or my actions, as a God who is passionately gracious and loving. This mistake resulted in a ministry that looked good from the outside, but did little to result in true heart change. I had been hitting the basics, but missing the basis.

the life changing affect of God's love

Think about love for a moment. Love has the power to change lives in incredible ways. It causes grown men to shop for flowers and teddy bears on February 13th. It causes women to give up the power of the remote control. It causes parents to drive to the pharmacy for children's cough syrup at two in the morning. Love causes a wife to try to work things out with an unfaithful husband. When love gets a hold of us, we become different people almost overnight—no convincing required. Our lives change because we have fallen under the control and the influence of love.

The same is true of one's relationship with Jesus Christ. I have come to realize that it is little use to tell a student how to follow Jesus without that student first falling madly in love with Jesus. Attempting to follow Christ without a love for him will almost always result in failure. We will always do what we deep down, really want to do. Unless our desires are changed by a genuine love for God—our sinful nature and sinful tendencies will always win out, and we will default back to our original sinful selves.

Add to this fact the truth John points out in 1 John 4:19, where he says that we will never fall in love with God until we realize his love for us. We love him because he first loved us. John tells us that this incredible love of God provides not only the *opportunity* for our loving response, but it provides the *motivation* as well.

John was just reiterating the truth he had mentioned earlier in the letter—God's love becomes our motivation for holiness and faithfulness. In 1 John he puts it this way:

> If we confess our sins, he is faithful and just and will forgive us our sins and purify us from all unrighteousness. If we claim we have not sinned, we make him out to be a liar and his word has no place in our lives. *My dear children, I write this to you so that you will not sin.* But if anybody does sin, we have one who speaks to the Father in our defense—Jesus Christ, the Righteous One. He is the atoning sacrifice for our sins, and not only for ours but also for the sins of the whole world (1 John 1:9-2:2).

1 John 1:9 was a verse that I had read countless times before, as was 1 John 2:1b. It was the important, little phrase in between them I had never noticed. Yet, in that little phrase, John explains to us exactly why he is writing these incredible truths.

In this passage John declares the extraordinary love of God. Because God loves us, he has gone to great lengths to forgive our sins and restore our relationship with him.

John begins with the certainty that if we confess our sins to God, God is faithful and will forgive us our sins. He continues on to tell us that is just the beginning. Even more amazing is the reality that even if we continue to sin, we have one who speaks on our behalf to the Father. This ensures that we will be forgiven not only of our sins in the past, but also all our sins in the future.

Right in between these two examples of God's love, John writes, "I write this to you so that you will not sin." The first time I actually noticed this quote, I couldn't help but be dumbfounded. On the surface it seemed out of place. John just told me that by simply confessing my sins, I can find complete forgiveness for every sin in my past and every sin in my future. How is this truth going to help me not sin? I thought to myself, "Won't it have just the opposite affect? How does the truth that all my sins are forgiven keep me from sinning? How does God's love motivate me to lead a pure life?" As quickly as the question surfaced, so did the answer. The answer came to me in a story that I passed on to my students that one Wednesday night.

a hypothetical situation

Imagine that you are a young man about to get engaged. You find yourself in the most unique of circumstances. You have the option of choosing between two young ladies. You are confident that either one of them will say "yes" and accept your proposal. You are faced with a difficult, important choice.

To make the decision even more difficult, the two young ladies happen to be identical twins, identical in almost every way. They look exactly the same. They have the same degree of intelligence. They have the same hobbies, interests, and goals. They both like to cook, do the dishes, change diapers, mow the lawn, shovel the snow, and change the oil (as long as we are being hypothetical, we might as well sweeten the deal). On the surface, there is nothing that separates one from the other. However, there is one thing that you have discovered about the women that is helpful information in choosing your future spouse. You know that Twin A loves you with an incredible love, and Twin B hates you with the same amount of passion.

Twin A loves you and wants nothing more than to give you the best life possible. She has a love for you that is unconditional, abundant, and extravagant—even to the point that she would give up everything, even her own life, to bring you joy and peace.

Twin B, on the other hand, hates you—legitimately hates you. She wants nothing more than to make your life miserable. And she is going to do whatever it takes to ultimately contribute to your death and destruction.

Now, with this additional piece of information, which young lady gets your wedding ring? Obviously, you are going to choose to marry the first. The decision has now become an easy one.

The Word of God and the reality of life make it clear that humans have only two options with their lives. We can choose to follow God or we can choose to follow the world and our sinful desires. We can choose to follow a God who loves us with an unconditional love or we can choose to chase after the world that offers temporal joy but eternal destruction. The decision may appear to be difficult at times as the world tries to lure us, but it is only hiding its true intent. The more we comprehend how much God loves us, the more apt we are to choose to follow him because we know that the one who loves us will lead us into real, lasting joy.

Every student sitting in your ministry, in your church, and on your school campus is faced everyday with the exact same decision. They are constantly bombarded with circumstances where they can choose to follow God or the world. The more your students understand, experience, and believe the abundance of God's love for them, the more they will choose him with their lives.

I tried for years to simply convince my students and their peers to choose Christ and follow him. It was not until I created a culture that constantly communicated God's love that I saw students eagerly choose to follow him. During that week, I stumbled upon what my ministry had been missing. It was the exact growth strategy used by Jesus, his apostles, and every writer in the New Testament. It was simply communicating the truth that God loves each and every single one of us!

creating a culture of love

I was talking to a pastor about this very thing. I was telling him about how much God had been teaching me about his love and the life-changing affect contained in that simple truth. I asked him if his church was intentional in communicating this to his people.

He said, "Yeah, of course we do."

I asked, "How do you specifically do that?"

He paused for a moment and then responded flippantly, "Well, we mention it."

I learned a little more that day about communicating God's love. I learned that communicating God's love effectively includes more than haphazardly "mentioning it." If I were to ask ten youth pastors if they were communicating God's love to students, I imagine I would get ten "yes, of course" responses. Indeed, even during those first four years of ministry, I would have answered yes to that question as well. I think I would have said, "Yeah, of course, I mention it all the time." But that is not enough.

I have learned that communicating God's love effectively and intentionally includes more than that. This truth needs to become the cornerstone that defines your ministry culture. Merely mentioning it from up front without allowing it to permeate everything you do creates an impression of a hollow, empty love that is often talked about but never realized.

So how does a youth leader create a culture of love in their ministry? I'll be the first to humbly admit that I do not get it right all the time and do not have all the answers (despite what my grandmother thinks of me). However, even without all the answers, I simply try as best I can to constantly create an atmosphere that champions God's love. Here are a few specific steps that I have found particularly helpful:

First, I remind myself that *God's love and grace cannot be communicated if they have not been experienced.* I will have little success establishing a culture of grace if I am not recognizing it in my own life. I have taken several identifiable steps to help me recognize God's grace in my life. I draw from experiences in my past that have led me to truly declare "only by the grace of God do I stand," and I have made a weekly discipline to meditate on God's love. Sitting quietly, I ask myself the same question I asked students years ago, "How have I specifically seen God show his love for me in the past week?" It has become a life altering discipline for me.

Second, I have made a point to not merely mention God's love, but to *systematically teach on the topic of God's love and grace.* Just like clockwork, you can set your watch to it. Once a year, in the fall, you can find me teaching on the love and grace of God. It doesn't end there. I come back to it again and again as the year unfolds. Even as we begin to tackle other relevant issues in a student's life, rarely will I let 6-8 weeks go by without coming back to the truth of God's love in some specific manner. It is a truth that needs to be constantly bombarded into our hearts and minds.

Third, I seek to *celebrate the little steps that students make.* Learning to follow Jesus doesn't happen overnight. It is a lifelong process filled with small steps along the way. If I hear of a small step taken (began reading their Bible, prayed out loud for the first time, went one week without swearing, etc.), I offer appropriate praise and encouragement to the student.

Fourth, I try *not to require more of Jesus followers than Jesus requires.* Yes, Jesus challenged his followers to follow him completely. Yet Jesus also famous for accepting and using people just as they were. As a matter of fact, some of the religious leaders of the day actually became upset with him at times (Luke 6:36ff). They couldn't believe the kinds of people that Jesus accepted into his kingdom. Jesus accepted them all, and he didn't expect them to become perfect overnight. Instead, he continued to show them love, grace, and patience. Look at Peter. After being around Jesus for three years and seeing some amazing things, Peter gave into temptation and denied ever knowing Jesus. How did Jesus respond? By putting Peter on probation? By requiring Peter to join an accountability group before he could go on the missions trip? No, he took him back immediately and put him to work for his kingdom. A culture of grace is a culture that accepts and uses students just as they are and does not require more of them than Jesus did.

Fifth, I *enjoy every second of it*! There is nothing more invigorating, exciting, and worthwhile than helping a student know that he or she is loved and accepted by God. Enjoy it too.

lemonade lessons

1. Close your eyes and meditate on this question: During the past week, in what real ways has God shown that he loves me?

2. As you look back at your life, how has God's love and grace played a role in your personal walk with Jesus Christ? What are some specific examples?

3. On a scale of 1 to 10, how would you rate your youth ministry in the area of "effectively communicating God's love to students?" Has this been accomplished intentionally or haphazardly?

4. Currently, in what specific ways does your youth ministry intentionally communicate God's love to students?

5. This chapter concluded with some specific steps that have been taken to champion God's love in a youth ministry; which of these specific steps are transferable to your ministry?

6. What would you add to this list? In what other practical ways can your youth ministry effectively champion God's love to students?

Steven Julian

So who reads a bio?

Most people don't read bio sheets in books, so you must want to know more about me or you want to know if I can help you in your ministry.

As for who I am—I am currently serving in Bozeman, Montana. I have been in youth ministry full-time for the last ten years and was a volunteer leader for four years prior to that. I am married to the most wonderful woman in the world—Stacey—and we are blessed with three beautiful boys—Joshua, Zach, and Elijah. We are a family who loves the baseball season to the utmost! I also enjoy the simple pleasures in life of a good meal, a good movie, or a good cup of coffee with a friend.

As for helping you . . . .My biggest passion in ministry centers on the concept of STORY! I have always enjoyed "talking shop" with youth workers while hearing and telling our stories. I have also enjoyed opportunities to tell MY STORY / THE STORY to teenagers and adults.

I would love to hear from you! Let me know how I can assist your ministry journey!

To contact Steven:
stevenmjulian@msn.com
406.587.4069

lemon 2

atomic elbows and Montana nights

(it's so much more than hype)

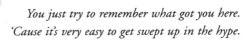

You just try to remember what got you here.
'Cause it's very easy to get swept up in the hype.

—Jimmy Smits

I have a confession I must make. I have chosen to reveal my secret in this book because this confession is CENTRAL and VITAL to the discussion we're having about leadership mistakes you can make in youth ministry. So, here goes . . . I am a closet fan of professional wrestling.

I can feel your shame for me. I can sense your awkwardness—having to read material from an ordained youth minister who still gets excited about atomic elbows from the top turnbuckle. However, the professional wrestling industry can teach us something about leadership, because it has survived and thrived due to one simple leadership concept . . . HYPE!

Professional wrestling is built almost entirely on hype. Just turn on any wrestling show. Within fifteen minutes you will hear about the latest betrayal of friends, the next newly invented match involving steel chairs, and the obligatory sales pitch for the next pay-per-view event along with thirteen reasons why you CANNOT MISS this great wrestling event. Of course, the ironic secret of wrestling hype is that two days after that pay-per-view is over, you will hear about the fifteen reasons why you cannot miss the NEXT great wrestling event in three weeks . . . also on pay-per-view!

So what do atomic elbows and figure four leg locks have to do with youth ministry leadership? I'm certainly not advocating "body slam Bible studies" or having a lock-in held in a steel cage. The point I'm trying to make is that I have been guilty of the same leadership and growth principles that professional wrestling has used for years. I have allowed my ministry to be LED BY HYPE rather than being LED BY LORDSHIP.

I have even given this ministry condition a name. I call it "Letting Hype Lead" Disorder, or LHL for short. Wrestling can get away with "Letting Hype Lead" because without it, their industry would collapse and everyone would see through the farce of fake wrestling. In ministry, we cannot allow LHL to creep in because it takes away from the true and genuine leadership of Jesus Christ.

> It destroys the soul to hear that you're all hype, that you have no talent, and that your whole career has been contrived.[2]
>
> – Freddie Mercury
> lead singer of Queen

OK, so you might be thinking that "Letting Hype Lead" is not a big problem in youth ministry. You might be thinking, "Hey, I bought this book to read about big mistakes I need to avoid like moral failure, burnout, and improper ministry tax deductions! Who cares about this LHL stuff?" Please don't skip to the next chapter or put the book down. I believe LHL is a serious and growing problem in North American youth ministry. It is a problem that affects all different types of ministries. It does not discriminate based on denomination, size of group, philosophy of ministry, genre of worship style, or even size of budget. I am a recovering LHL youth pastor who wants to help you face this problem by defining the problem, looking at some of the symptoms, and going through a leadership treatment plan.

. . . so where do we start?

First, we must ask, "Is there anything inherently wrong with hype?" As the Apostle Paul would say, "May it never be!" I do not believe that hype, in and of itself, is a sin. With proper usage, hype can be a very good thing. Getting students excited about an upcoming event which results in them inviting friends is a good thing. Talking repeatedly and excitedly about a new CD single that leads to deeper interest in encouraging music is a great thing. Getting "hyped up" about the spiritual decisions of students is a natural response of a healthy ministry.

The problem is not with hype itself. The problem is when we are led down the path of the "Letting Hype Lead" Disorder. When hype has moved from a tool to an idol, then hype has moved to a position of improper leadership. When hype is no longer one element of your ministry and is now the defining trait of your ministry, then you have an unhealthy LHL disorder. When hype has moved from a byproduct that flows out of your honest efforts to an obsession that drives you for your next hype-fix as the leader, then you need help.

So what are the symptoms of the LHL disorder? What should we be watching out for as we try to stay away from the path of "Letting Hype Lead?"

symptom #1: hyping the stats

"How many students come to your youth ministry?"

"How many students made decisions last year through your youth ministry?"

"How many students vomited last year due to your game times?"

Numbers matter. Numbers count. I do NOT want to dispute or argue about the validity of numbers in ministry. I DO want to discuss the issue of "Letting Hype Lead" in the arena of numbers. In my struggles with LHL, POPULATION becomes more important than the PEOPLE of my ministry. My thirst to add five more students leads to a lust for ten more students. Breaking the twenty person barrier becomes a prideful desire to break

Do Numbers Matter?

• Jesus fed 5,000 people (Matthew 14:21), which means they were counting their "dining customers." The disciples even counted how many baskets of food were left over!

• The disciples counted 3,000 people who accepted Christ as Savior on the day of Pentecost (Acts 2:41).

• God had Moses count the people of Israel multiple times on their trip to the promised land. . . . Heck, they even included a book from that story called "Numbers" in the canon of Scripture!

the forty person barrier. Numbers are important, but they should never become more important than the faces and the lives that those numbers represent.

The manifestation of this symptom normally shows up first with names. I have never been good at remembering names, but I have always made the effort because I realize the importance of someone feeling recognized. On more than one occasion I have gotten so wrapped up with my numbers that I display a lack of concern for learning names of students. I'm more excited about the five visitors that gave us a new attendance-record than I am about the stories of these five unique people whom God has placed in my path. I caution all youth leaders to keep vigilant watch over the balance between attendance on a report and attention to a life.

symptom #2: hyping the comp

Ministry is not a competition. We are not trying to win a contest like "American Idol—Youth Leaders Edition!" There are no "Youth Ministry Standings" in the Monday morning paper for me to see where I rank while drinking my morning coffee. Yet, as I examine this second symptom, I realize that more than once I have been caught in the trap of seeing youth ministry as a competition. Competition among ministries can create a hype-induced frenzy of negative results.

Let us set the record straight again. Ministering to youth is a CALLING, not a COMPETITION. I am called to join God in His mission of reaching teenagers with the gospel of Jesus Christ. I am called to be involved in the discipleship process among the lives of teenagers. I am called to nurture, shepherd, and send students out to follow Jesus and join Him in His work.

However, my sinful nature can still fall prey to twinges of jealousy and envy of the "cool church" on the other side of town. You know the church I'm talking about. They are the church with the big youth budget and the worship band that just cut a new CD. The church that just opened the new youth center-complete with internet café, climbing wall, and virtual reality tours of the Holy Land!

So you try to block their good fortune and blessing from your mind. You tell yourself that you are more holy and sanctified as you "suffer" with your Nintendo 64™ and your semi-tattered thrift store couches. Yet you can't help but hope that you draw more students to your church's outreach event. You try not to smile when a parent tells you how much more "authentic" your ministry is for their teenagers. Pretty soon you are in full blown LHL "competition" mode.

Youth leaders, we must avoid the hype of competition. We must not allow the enemy a foothold in our relationships with other churches and other leaders who have the same passion for students, relationships, and discipleship that we do! Become an agent of coming together instead of competing apart.

symptom #3: hyping the gimmick

We live in a world of instant gratification. Teenagers are the biggest supporters and addicts of the "give it to me now" society. I begin to give in to their unhealthy immediate

---

Gimmicks You Haven't Seen Advertised . . . Yet!

- "Use our curriculum and in thirteen weeks your group will be full of certified saints!"

- "This five week study on Leviticus will have your students wearing ephods in no time!"

- "Sell this box of t-shirts and entire nations will be saved while you earn 5% commission for your group!"

desires when I let hype lead. In so doing, I trade the process and journey of deeper spiritual growth for the immediate results of the latest gimmick.

There is nothing wrong with curriculums, Bible studies, and positive T-shirts. My LHL mistake has been to let the GIMMICK take the place of true GROWTH. My mistake has been when I see a new curriculum as a quick gimmick that will bring quick spiritual results instead of letting the process happen separate from my desires and hype. I want kids to be excited about God, not my gimmicks. I need to stop chasing the next big thing and follow the REAL big thing.

. . . so how do you fight this LHL disorder?

You read most books like this to get answers. You hope the author can provide an "A-HA!" moment for you. You expect me to give you the "Seven Habits of Purpose Driven Hype-Busting" which will keep you from falling into the LHL disorder.

However, I believe LHL is not completely curable. There is no magic drug or sermon series that will completely eliminate LHL from our leadership lives. I do believe there is a treatment plan, that if diligently followed daily, can stop the spread of LHL. There is certainly nothing novel or new about this plan. In fact, what we need is right in front of us, waiting to be recognized again.

Montana nights

Two years ago I accepted a position at a church in Montana. I had never been in the vicinity of Montana before coming out for my interview weekend with my wife, but I had heard the stories of Montana being nicknamed "Big Sky Country." On one night of our trip, my wife and I discovered why Montana got that nickname. We stood on a driveway in the foothills of the Madison mountain range with our heads tilted back and our mouths wide open. We stood there speechless on that chilly December night looking up at millions of stars, more than we had ever seen. My wonder and amazement led to a renewed worship of my Almighty

Creator. That Montana sky reminded me again of God's power, creativity, and majesty—wonderful traits of the best leader around.

The treatment plan for the LHL disorder is to "Let Jesus Lead." You combat LHL with LJL! Just like the Montana night sky, Jesus is all around us. The power and the presence of our Creator and Savior are always nearby. We serve a God who is not far away, yet he will never impose his will or his leadership upon us. Jesus is powerful and loving enough to let us choose how we lead or are led. So how do we combat the LHL disorder with the LJL cure? How have I combated my disorder and seen growth, victory, and balance?

> When I look at your heavens, the creation of your fingers, the moon and the stars that you have set in place—what is a mortal that you remember him or the Son of Man that you take care of him?
>
> – Psalm 8:3-4
> "God's Word" Version

let Jesus lead in you

I grew up hearing about Jesus needing to be "the Lord of my life." This truly means that he is in charge. He is the head of the manor and I am his loyal serf! I must deal with who is leading on a personal level first. Any change in the leadership of our youth ministries must flow out of a change in the leadership of our lives.

Spend some time meditating on the urgency of Paul's instruction. Our lives must be offered as a "living sacrifice." Once we place ourselves on that altar, Jesus can truly lead, guide, and direct our lives. We must start the LJL treatment by asking who is in charge of our lives daily. Are you letting Jesus lead or are you taking back control by getting off the altar to do your own thing? This treatment calls for daily getting on the altar and letting Jesus lead IN us first.

let Jesus lead around you

"Letting Hype Lead" is usually a self-promotion bonanza. We take all the credit and the glory for what we've done. We believe that the story is all about us. As the LJL treatment plan begins to work on the inside, we begin to open our eyes to the world around us. We begin to see other people who inhabit that world. We begin to see that Jesus wants to lead more than our own lives. Jesus wants to lead around our lives as well.

Our world gets bigger as our God gets bigger. We do not allow hype to lead us for our own gains of self-promotion. We allow Jesus to lead us to our new story that's not about us and is all about Him. Look around and ask, "Is Jesus leading AROUND my life?"

let Jesus lead through you

The LJL treatment plan can lead you down amazing paths. The tempting draw of "Letting Hype Lead" is to accomplish some "stuff" in ministry. You get more people. You do more events. You generate more excitement. However, when the LJL treatment plan begins to steer you to the leadership of Christ in your life, and when your eyes are opened to the way Jesus leads around you, then you are on the threshold of some amazing leadership results. You are about to see Jesus lead THROUGH you.

Hebrews 12:1-2 tells us that we should "fix our eyes on Jesus." This is the job of the Holy Spirit. As we let Jesus lead us, he fills us with the Holy Spirit to point us toward him and toward the work that he is doing around us. Then the "mystery

> Brothers and sisters, in view of all we have just shared about God's compassion, I encourage you to offer your bodies as living sacrifices, dedicated to God and pleasing to him. This kind of worship is appropriate for you. Don't become like the people of this world. Instead, change the way you think. Then you will always be able to determine what God really wants—what is good, pleasing, and perfect.
>
> – Romans 12:1-2
> "God's Word" Version

of ministry" happens as Jesus allows us to be a part of the amazing things he is doing all around us. Jesus uses us to reach students. Jesus lets us see the spiritual transformations of teenagers responding, following, and serving their Savior. Jesus changes the world around us and even uses our talents, gifts, and abilities to do it! Jesus leads THROUGH us, and the world is changed forever!

So, if you want to avoid my biggest mistake in youth ministry, don't let hype lead you. You know something . . . there was a temptation on my part to try and write this chapter with hype leading me. I was tempted to write a big story with a big conflict and a big solution that would lead to big sales. Yet, in the end, the solution is not anything new. Let the Lord lead you as his name implies. Let the Lordship of Christ create leadership opportunities in you, around you, and through you. . . . That is, unless you're interested in buying my next "Most Amazing Youth Ministry Leadership Lessons" class on pay-per-view. It just might be the greatest pay per view youth ministry event of all time!

> Since we are surrounded by so many examples of faith, we must get rid of everything that slows us down, especially sin that distracts us. We must run the race that lies ahead of us and never give up. We must focus on Jesus, the source and goal of our faith. He saw the joy ahead of him, so he endured death on the cross and ignored the disgrace it brought him. Then he received the highest position in heaven, the one next to the throne of God.
>
> – Hebrews 12:1-2
> "God's Word" Version

lemonade lessons

1. Have you ever let HYPE lead your ministry? Have you seen the three symptoms creep up around your youth ministry?

2. Are there any other symptoms you would recognize that contribute to an LHL disorder in your youth ministry?

3. How is Jesus leading IN you right now? What is he asking you to do or to change in your life right now?

4. How is Jesus leading AROUND you right now? Take a few minutes and think about the people, the circumstances, and the opportunities that Jesus is in the midst of around your life right now? Where can you join him in that work?

5. Are you letting Jesus lead THROUGH you right now? What "God-stuff" have you seen spill out of your life lately?

Andy Geffers

Andy has been involved in youth ministry for over 12 years. He is currently Pastor of Student Ministries at Church of Emmanuel in Foxboro, Massachusetts, where he has been serving for over six years. He is a graduate of Nyack College and has a Masters Degree in Public Administration from John Jay College, New York City. Andy has been happily married to his wife, Holly, for 20 years and has two children, Andrew and Elizabeth. They enjoy vacationing, biking, playing football games in the living room, and watching the Patriots! Andy is a leader whose desire is to be used by God to influence others to Love Jesus, Live Jesus and Lead for Jesus. He also has a passion for helping youth ministries and leaders excel and take the leap to the next level of effectiveness. He has been a seminar leader at conferences and has spoken at local churches. Andy loves books, spending time with his family, and hanging with teenagers at local restaurants and school events. He is a sports fanatic and has recently become addicted to fantasy leagues.

To contact Andy:
reverendandy5@yahoo.com
508.813.8640

God, are you sure you want me?

(being the leader God created you to be)

The Creator of the universe built you to be a creative expression of himself.

—Erwin McManus

You are a leader! Different, perhaps; but just as "created" as other, more "natural" leaders.

It took me a long time to come to the point where I believed that statement. It has only been within the last few years that I have come to believe that God created me to be a leader. My personality is more reserved (or very reserved, depending on who is scoring). Despite being on the quiet side, I kept finding myself in leadership roles asking God, "Why do you keep directing me to leadership positions when you have not given me the gift or skills of leadership I see in others?"

Have you ever felt that way? Do you feel that way now? Maybe you are not reserved, but "too old." Perhaps you feel too young, too inexperienced, not funny enough, not cool enough, not pretty enough, not

_____ enough. If so, this chapter is for you! I do not fit a "classic" leader or youth worker personality. But God has taken me on a long and fulfilling journey of discovery that has taught me to trust in how he has created me. God has created you unique and intends to use your uniqueness to make you the kind of leader he designed you to be.

my story

In 1994, I earned a masters degree in Public Administration. I obtained my degree by attending a program on the campus of West Point: the United States Army's premier leadership training school. As I observed young cadets, I would think to myself, "Now those are real leaders!" My classes were filled with future police and fire chiefs, as well as those who would go on to be government leaders for entire cities and towns. I knew that I was not like these people.

To make things worse, my first leadership job ended in failure. I still remember the feelings. I was hurt, broken, defeated, and lost. I was full of questions. Why did this happen? Was it my fault? Was I a failure? What am I good at? Will I ever be successful? This was a real breaking point for me that began a journey of discovery and restoration. God taught me a huge, but basic lesson: "You can't do anything

> Hope comes not from making our lives more comfortable but from discovering great visions.[3]
>
> – M. Craig Barnes
> author of _Sacred Thirst_

without me!" It wasn't that I didn't know that in my head, but it was like God spoke it right into my heart that day. I remember it as if it were yesterday.

After wrestling hard over the direction my life and career should take, God opened the door for . . . you guessed it; another, even more challenging leadership position. It was basically doing the same thing that I had just failed at, but this time with increased responsibility. I worked successfully (but not confidently) administrating group homes for adults with autism and other special needs for the next four years. At the time I left, I was supervising nine homes, the building and maintenance department, and one administrative assistant. Even in the church I was attending, I was fulfilling two leadership positions. It often felt like I could not escape God's plan for using and developing me as a leader.

Then, six and a half years ago, the opportunity came for me to enter full-time ministry as a youth pastor. It did not take long for me to discern that God was calling me to this. I still did not feel that I was a "created" leader. I continued to question God, a lot: "Are you sure you want me God? I am the reserved one, remember? Are you sure you want me to stand up in front of people and talk? Are you sure you want me to unite a team? Don't you have other, more 'natural' people who can do it better?" Does this sound like any Bible characters you remember? Moses, right! God has used the life of Moses to teach me a lot about myself, a lot about leadership and most of all a lot about trust.

trust in your uniqueness

Moses struggled when he failed to realize that God had created him unique for a reason. Moses was a reluctant leader who questioned his ability to speak effectively. I have struggled most, when like Moses, I have questioned if God made a mistake either in his creation of me or in his instructions. You will struggle less when you gain confidence that God has created you just the way he wanted to. I looked at the classic youth worker—young, funny, outgoing, and certainly not reserved—and recognized that I was not that youth worker. This led me to question if I could be an effective youth worker or a leader of youth workers when I clearly don't look or act like them? What was God's response to Moses when he asked similar questions? God basically said, "Moses, I know you don't speak well, but that is how I created you. I'm not worried, why are you? Would I have asked you to do this if I didn't think (and since it was God, *know*) you could do it?" How often do we doubt God's creation? Do you ever doubt yourself? God has created you to be just the person he wanted you to be.

> The Creator of the universe built you to be a creative expression of himself.[4]
>
> – Erwin McManus
> author of *Uprising*

Later in the book of Exodus, we get a glimpse of what God had in mind when he created Moses. Moses came down the mountain where God had given him the Ten Commandments. He then dropped (ok, smashed) them when he encountered Aaron and all the people worshiping a golden calf. God was ready to leave Israel to wander alone in the wilderness, but Moses intervened. He went to the tent of meeting where, as Exodus 33:10 says, "The Lord would speak to Moses face to face, as a man speaks with his friend." A few verses later Moses says, "If your Presence does not go with us, do not send us up from here. How will anyone know that you are pleased with me and with your people unless you go with us?" Look at the positives of Moses' temperament. First, he had a regular habit of meeting with God in the "tent of Meeting" to the point where God would speak to him as a man would a friend. Second, Moses knew enough not to head off on a journey without the assurance of God being with him because he recognized that he was nothing without God. Do you see why God created Moses just the way he was? God needed someone who would not wander from him and seek other gods when things got tough. Why? Because God knew he was going to lead a whole nation that had a strong tendency to do just that.

In recent years I have begun to recognize more clearly that God has given me a unique personality, a unique skill set, unique passions, and unique gifts. According to Jeremiah 29:11, God created me unique because he knew the plans he had for me. I have witnessed God use my uniqueness again and again for his purpose. I have been able to build a solid, growing, and intentional ministry. I have not done this through my great sense of humor, "life of the party" personality, or good looks! But God has worked through my uniqueness to accomplish this. He has used my reserved personal-

> I have witnessed God use my uniqueness again and again for his purpose.

ity to keep me steady. I have been able to stay in my current ministry for six years now working out God's plan for these students. He has given me one on one relational skill that allows people to feel truly cared about. This has made our youth group one that ministers to many students who need special care and are often rejected in other peer groups. God has given me a deep passion to see students' lives transformed. This passion has kept this ministry active, intentional, and forward moving. Whether counseling teens and families, speaking, shepherding, or helping others, my gifts are just what God wanted to use in this place at this time.

trust in God's promise to equip us

Don't hear what I am not saying. I am not saying that it is okay not to work on areas that are changeable. For all we know God's plan for Moses may have involved some speech classes and maybe even anger management! But would Moses ever become an eloquent, knock-your-socks-off speaker? Probably not. But if he was put in a situation where that was needed, I know God would have equipped him to do what was needed. I know this because that is exactly what God has done in my life and ministry.

> God's plan for Moses may have involved some speech classes and maybe even anger management!

Often I have been faced with situations where I needed to be adequate, or even very good, and God has equipped me to do what needed to be done. This has been true generally and in specific situations through out my life.

God has never stopped equipping me, whether it is has been a time when I needed his wisdom to give advice to a struggling student, leading to discern the next step to move the ministry forward, or the ability to stay up all night trying to keep up with junior highers. When God calls you to do something, he has promised to equip you to do it.

When I started in youth ministry, I was not a gifted speaker. Over time, however, I have been equipped by God and do a pretty good job (at least that is what people tell me) at teaching and preaching. Will I ever be on television? Probably not. But God has not called me to television? Probably not. All I know is I can be a very effective speaker when God has something to say through me.

A funny example of God's equipping me happened during a camping trip. It was one of those trips that involved tents, about 40 junior high students, and rain! Not a good combination! But it got worse. Thunder and lots of lightning began to arrive just when our main activities were to begin. We decided to jump in the cars and head into town. Basically the town consisted of a gas station and a grocery store. At that moment I needed some equipping and God came through. He helped me be creative in a moment when I needed to be creative. He gave me the idea of breaking the 40 students into groups, giving each group a one dollar bill (yes, I am cheap!), and a challenge to find the best purchase for one dollar. It went great, and everyone had a blast; except the store manager, of course! I was really surprised the next year when, before the trip, several students asked, "Are we going to do that grocery store thing again?" That experience and many others are reminders that God will equip me and you when he asks us to do something, and his stuff is always better than ours.

> Do not worry about how you will defend yourself or what you will say, for the Holy Spirit will teach you at the time what you should say.
>
> – Luke 12:11b-12

we must trust in God's ability to transform us

How did Moses go from the man who resisted God's call to be a leader, to a man who led an entire nation who wanted to turn back and become slaves again by saying, "Do not be afraid. Stand firm and you will see the deliverance the Lord will bring you today" (Exodus 14:13)? How did he lead them into a sea that just happened to part as he took his staff and stretched it out over the water? How was he able to become a respected leader who remained in leadership for over 40 years? Moses was able, through God's intervention, to actually be transformed on the inside from a servant to a leader. When I look at my life and specifically, my ministry, I can see that not only has God equipped me along the way, he has been transforming me on the inside into the leader he has created me to be. No matter what your position—full-time, part-time, or volunteer—God has placed you where you are. He has a plan for you, and that plan begins with getting you to recognize that your role is to be a leader. Maybe you are to lead children, youth, adults, or even other leaders. Maybe you are to lead one, 100, or even 1,000. What, or how many, you lead is second-ary to how you lead. You see, God wants you to *BE* a leader before he wants you to *DO* leadership.

For me this meant that I needed to allow God to show me that I was a leader. My tendency when I first began youth ministry was to rely on others to lead. It was easy to look to more experienced people for leader-

> God wanst you to *BE* a leader be-fore he wants you to *DO* leadership.

ship. They often looked a lot more like leaders than me. But I needed to come to the point where I responded to the need for leadership by being a leader myself. I needed God to begin to transform me so that I could see myself as a leader. I needed to pray as a leader, study as a leader, and plan as a leader. Only God can transform a person into an effective leader so that he believes it on the inside. He did it with Moses and many oth-ers. Listen to what Amos says about himself in Amos 7:14-16a when a priest told him to stop prophesying. "I was neither a prophet nor a prophet's son, but I was a shepherd, and I also took care of sycamore-fig trees. But the Lord took me from tending the flock and said to me, 'Go, prophesy to my people Israel.' Now then hear the word of the Lord." Amos had been transformed! Don't you love how he ends: "Now then hear the word of the Lord"? Amos was so convinced that God had trans-formed him into a prophet that he responded to the very person who was telling him to stop by basically saying, "Look, I know you are the high-est religious figure in the nation, but God made me a prophet, so shut up and listen!" Again, I feel the need for a disclaimer. I'm not giving you

> Don't become so well-adjusted to your culture that you fit into it without even thinking. Instead, fix your attention on God. You'll be changed from the inside out. Readily recognize what he wants from you, and quickly respond to it. Unlike the culture around you, always dragging you down to its level of immaturity, God brings the best out of you, develops well-formed maturity in you. I'm speaking to you out of deep gratitude for all that God has given me, and especially as I have responsibilities in relation to you. Living then, as every one of you does, in pure grace, it's important that you not misinterpret yourselves as people who are bringing this goodness to God. No, God brings it all to you. The only accurate way to understand ourselves is by what God is and by what he does for us, not by what we are and what we do for him.
>
> – Romans 12:2-3
> *The Message*

permission to say that to your pastor the next time he fails to agree that your new idea was given to you directly by God. But seriously, if you are going to lead, you must trust in God's ability to transform you on the inside and take steps to allow him to do it.

getting practical

Okay, let's get practical. What does this mean to you? Here are just a few suggestins that will help you be the leader God created you to be.

Spend time discovering how you were created unique. This is the first step. If you are not sure how you are created unique, it is very important for you to figure that out. There are many books and websites that help you with discovering your spiritual gifts, skills, and passions. Talk with the people around you that you trust to give you honest feedback. They can be great resources in helping you discover your uniqueness.

Plan ahead for your weaknesses. This involves two things. First, things that you will never be able to do well need to be filled in by recruiting others who do those things well. Second, areas where you can improve must be given time and effort so that you become adequate in those areas. It is just as important to know your weaknesses as it is to know your strengths.

Find the right "fit." Certain personalities work well together, others do not. Certain responsibilities will fit your uniqueness, others will not. The better the fit at the beginning, the better your uniqueness can be used by God. Spend lots of time seeking God's wisdom when choosing a place to serve.

Recognize your place of leadership. I will probably never be a CEO of a fortune 500 company. I probably won't be a leader of a mega-church. I may never be a "top" leader in any organization. My uniqueness often makes me most effective as a "second chair" leader. I think it is important not to see this as a vertical scale, but as a horizontal menu. The place God has prepared for you and your uniqueness is exactly where you should be. Sometimes "moving up" may not be moving "up" but "away" from where God desires you to be. If God desires you to look at the leadership menu and choose to be a CEO, then that is what you should go after. If God desires you to choose to be a middle manager, then that is what you should go after. God has created you unique and wants you to fill a unique leadership role.

And finally, *remember you are a leader!* You won't lead exactly the way I lead. If you did, neither of us would be unique. God has made you special and has places where he wants to use you just the way he created you. He did it with Moses, and he wants to do it with you.

Recommended Resources:

- www.leadingfromyourstrengths.com (they have assessment tools that help you identify your strengths)
- *Next Generation Leaders* by Andy Stanley
- *Leading From the Second Chair* by Mike Bonem & Roger Patterson
- *The Gift of Being Yourself* by David G. Benner

lemonade lessons

1. What doubts about yourself and your leadership are you holding on to?

2. How has God created you unique?

3. How have you seen God use your uniqueness?

4. What are your weaknesses? Who could fill in your gaps?

5. How has God equipped you in the past?

6. Is transformation beginning inside you? If so, how are you starting to see yourself as a leader? What can you do to begin or continue this transformation?

7. What kind of leadership role do you think God has created you to fill?

8. Is your current situation a good fit? Are you sure your answer is not based on temporary circumstances?

Jay Abiera

Jay is currently serving as youth pastor for Alliance Bible Church of Downey (ABCD) in California and has been in youth ministry for over 11 years. He attended Talbot School of Theology in La Mirada, California, and graduated with a Master of Arts in Christian Education in 2000. Besides being the youth pastor for ABCD, he is also the National Director for Youth Ministries for the Association of Filipino Churches of the Christian and Missionary Alliance (C&MA). He participates in district and national youth ministries and has coordinated several youth conferences. Pastor Jay has a heart and passion to reach teens for Jesus Christ and to help them grow and mature in their relationship with Him. Pastor Jay has been married to his wife, Charmaine, for four years.

To contact Jay:
jayabiera@gmail.com

lemon 4

I got this!

(leaving God out of the success equation)

We can ever remain powerless . . . by trying to do God's work not in concentration on His power, but by ideas drawn from our own temperament.[5]

—Oswald Chambers

In my senior year of college, while studying to be a physical therapist, God called me to full-time youth ministry. I didn't hear crazy voices or anything, but after months of seeking him and through a series of Godly events, I was certain that he was calling me to minister specifically to Filipino-American teenagers, or second generation Filipino-Americans. I was passionate about the calling that God placed in my heart, and I was excited to have a significant, meaningful mission in my life. I gave up the whole physical therapy thing, basically tossing out my degree, and signed up for seminary.

I wanted to learn everything I could about youth ministry. In seminary, I was pushed and challenged to know more about God. I learned how to study him better through his Word, and I picked up some tools to help me pursue my calling. My training exposed me to successful youth ministry models at other churches. I learned about the whole "Purpose Driven Youth Ministry" thing from Saddleback Church in Lake Forest, California. I learned about youth ministries at churches like Willow Creek and went through Sonlife Training. When I graduated from seminary, I fully expected to take the tools I learned and the training I received to pursue the ministry God gave me and save the world.

I started working at a Filipino church with no youth ministry. I was excited about starting fresh with no real expectations and without "ministry messes" to clean up. At this point, I was confident. It seemed as if I had all the ingredients for my ministry to succeed. I had my seminary training, the right church ministry, and the perfect plan to make it all work. All I needed to do was implement my plan and watch young, lost, Filipino-American teenagers be blown away by God's message, fall to their knees, and commit their lives to Jesus Christ.

Unfortunately, it didn't happen as I planned. My first two years of full-time youth ministry were a failure. I was enthusiastic and optimistic heading into the ministry, but after those first two years, I was extremely disappointed. I worked diligently to implement the vision I had for this ministry, but it just seemed nothing was working. When I started I had five students, but two years down the road, I added exactly one teenager to my youth ministry. That's right . . . one—and he was the brother of one of the original five.

After putting in all the work possible to make this ministry succeed, I felt like a major failure. We weren't bringing in new students. We didn't really lead anyone to Christ. And it seemed like the students we did have weren't truly growing in their relationship with God. After just the first couple of years in the ministry, I was exhausted, frustrated, and confused. I saw no success in what I was doing. I felt like a complete failure.

I found myself doubting every part of my ministry. I began really thinking about quitting. I felt like maybe I could better serve and glorify God in a secular occupation and still be involved in youth ministry. However, in the face of my failure as a pastor, I devoted time in the Word and went to God in prayer asking him for answers and realized *he* was the answer all along. I realized my foolish mistake: *I relied too much on my own abilities.* I leaned on my training and education for the answers to ministry success. Furthermore, I learned that as a youth worker I shouldn't have sought my own standard of ministry success. In other words, I shouldn't seek out the *world's* standard of ministry success. I should, more than anything, seek out God.

During the early years of my ministry, I focused on being a "successful" youth pastor. This isn't necessarily a bad thing. Who doesn't want to be successful? But many times as youth workers, and as Christians in general, we measure success using the world's standards. Success in God's eyes can look much different.

By the world's standard, success in ministry is measured by three words: numbers, numbers, numbers. It's all about the digits. We tend to define the success of our individual ministries solely by the number of people involved in it. How often are we asked about our ministries, and we answer with a number? At the end of the year, how do we evaluate the health of our ministries? Is it by the number of students that show up? Using this standard in my early ministry proved to be a complete failure.

The more I sought out God, though, the more I realized that my standard for success wasn't the same as God's standards. How can we be successful in God's eyes? Isn't that what it's really all about?

a successful foundation

I went to a seminar years ago for some youth ministry training. It was probably one of the first youth ministry training events I'd ever attended. The seminar was a long time ago, but I still remember this one phrase: "Momentum kills intimacy."

The phrase was referring to the success we experience in ministry, and the excitement we feel when we experience some "success." As we gain momentum through this suc-

> Put first things first and we get second things thrown in: Put second things first and we lose both first and second things.[6]
>
> – Wayne Martindale
> author of *The Quotable Lewis*

cess, our natural reaction is to build on that momentum. We want to take what happens, and the success that it brings, and build on it so that we can gain more success.

However, if we look at the life of Jesus Christ, he didn't follow this principle. When he experienced "success" and popularity in his earthly ministry, Jesus didn't go, he stopped. When Jesus saw success in his ministry, Jesus paused. He did what seemed like the last thing you would do when things are going well. Instead of getting up, planning more, and working harder, Jesus took the time to connect with God. He paused and spent a great deal of time in solitude in order to refresh himself and find solace in his Father.

I believe the attitude Jesus used to approach his ministry is one that we need to use in our own ministries. I know the feeling of excitement when you see a ministry grow. I understand that feeling of elation when you give a great talk and kids respond with excitement and brokenness. I've been in youth ministry long enough to experience the highs that it can bring, but I've also realized that those highs come and go.

As youth leaders, we have to understand that our success isn't determined by our numbers, it's determined by our ability to stay intimately connected to our Father in Heaven. Jesus was never really impressed with the number of followers he had. He wasn't seduced by that type of success. That wasn't where his sense of mission and accomplishment came from. No matter how popular Jesus became, his mission came from his Father, and he never lost sight of

> We slander God by our very eagerness to work for Him without knowing Him.[7]
>
> – Oswald Chambers
> author of *My Utmost for His Highest*

that. He never allowed his popularity to fool him into thinking he was a success. His relationship with his Father is what made him successful.

This is a lesson and a discipline that I've had to learn and develop over and over again in my ministry. It's really easy for me to get into my work. It's really easy for me to get so caught up with what needs to be done instead of focusing on what REALLY needs to be done. What's more, when

I experience momentum or success in my ministry, my first reaction is to jump on it so that I can build on the success that I see. This isn't necessarily a bad thing; it's just not the most important thing. Of course, we want to be prudent with our time and resources so we can invest in the things that are working. However, we must never forget that the most important thing for us to do is pause and stay connected with our Father in heaven.

It is through him that we are able to understand his Word. It is through him that true success in ministry (and in life) is found. And ultimately, it is through our relationship with him that we will truly find success, not just in our respective ministries, but also in our lives as his disciples. Success in life really depends on this relationship. Let's not get so caught up with trying to find ministry success by the world's standard, but instead always keep our focus and find eternal success in our relationship with him.

the power of success

We live in a very result-centered society. To be successful, we want to see results. We want to see lives changed. If there aren't results, we tend to label things as unsuccessful and see ourselves as failures. We have to remember, though, that lives change not by our magical words or by our youth ministry skills and talents, but by the power of the Holy Spirit. The power of success comes from him.

We may feel like a failure as we minister to a student and get little or no response; but remember, this is a supernatural process. When it seems like there's nothing going on externally, there may be a lot going on internally. Without your knowledge, God may be working in the heart of the teenager, convicting him and revealing himself to him. Don't go by what you see. Let God work and put your faith in the fact that you are doing what God wants you to be doing. I believe that as you faithfully prepare your lessons and minister to the best of your abilities,

> It is possible to move men through God by prayer alone.[8]
>
> – Hudson Taylor
> missionary to China
> founder of China Inland Mission

you are already a success. Your success or failure isn't defined by this kid responding to God (that's ultimately between God and the teenager). Your success has already been found in the joy of an intimate, personal relationship with your almighty, all-powerful God.

In Mark 9, Jesus performed an exorcism that his disciples were unable to perform. After exorcising the demon, Jesus' disciples asked him why they couldn't do it. Jesus' response was simple, yet profound: "This kind can come out only by prayer."

The disciples relied on their skills, training, and past experiences. They figured that their past success had prepared the way for their future success. But true ministry success doesn't happen out of our strength. Our skills and abilities have very little to do with changing a life. That kind of success, that kind of change, can only come from the power of God.

I've been in youth ministry for over 10 years and there's one important lesson that I continue to learn throughout my ministry. It is that I have very little to do with changing a student's life. The more I'm involved with ministry, the more I realize that successful ministry has very little to do with me. I am Christ's servant. I can't take any credit. He is the only one that can change lives.

> Until you have prayed, you can do nothing but pray. Once you have prayed, you can do so much more than pray!
>
> – Ron Compass
> AIM missionary

As a pastor, I know that my words and my appeals are simply not enough. I know that there are times when the best thing I can do for students is just to stop and pray for them. It may seem unproductive. It may seem as if I'm not doing enough to bring about success in ministry, but praying is exactly what Jesus did to be successful. And if Jesus relied on the power of prayer and the power of his Father in heaven to find success in ministry, how much more do I need to rely on this?

The power for success in ministry is not from my skills or talents, nor is it from programs and ministry models. The power for success in youth ministry comes only from him. I value this lesson because it keeps me humble. Through my mistakes and failures, I realize that ministry success comes only from him. He is the only one that can change lives.

a success story

Leah is a bright, bubbly girl who grew up in the church where I serve. She was raised in a Christian home and has always valued the Christian life. I could tell, though, that as much as she valued being a Christian, she valued the world just as much. I knew there was a big part of her that wanted all that this world had to offer a teenage girl: popularity, boyfriends, and partying with friends. As she entered high school, these things became just as valuable to her as her Christianity.

Then one day, sometime before her sophomore year in high school, Leah approached me with conviction in her heart; she wanted to be right with God and

> God doesn't call us to be successful; he calls us to be faithful.[9]
>
> – Anonymous

be completely committed to him. She shared with me what she was going through, and I prayed with her, reminding her how much God truly loved her. I sensed she was broken as a sinner in the presence of her Holy God. At that moment, I knew that God had worked miraculously in her life, and that her heart was changed. God worked to show her that she was on a destructive path, and she recognized what God had to offer her was so much more fulfilling. I knew then that she was changed completely.

Since then, I've seen Leah continue to grow as a Christian. She serves faithfully as a student leader and is active in reaching out to her friends at school. I'm sure she still has her ups and downs, but God continues to work to transform her heart as she passionately pursues him.

After some time, Leah wrote me a letter to thank me for helping her. She wrote:

I want to thank you so much for everything you have taught me. You have been such a great supporter, helper, and teacher. You have always been there for me. I thank God for the gift he has given you. Without you asking me questions all the time, talking to me, knowing what's up in my life; without you being our youth pastor, without you picking me up, without you helping me through ministry, without you just BEING THERE, I wouldn't be the person I am now. I really, really want to thank you for EVERYTHING. You've seen me cry, get angry, get hurt, and everything. You know my troubles and you find ways to help me feel better.

Reading this letter, I was very touched and grateful for the opportunity to minister to Leah. I was also very humbled. I know me. I'm not all that. I knew that what happened was that God got a hold of Leah's heart, and she surrendered to him. I prayed for her and ministered to her as best as I could, but it was God who truly worked to change Leah's heart.

At the end of the day as youth workers, we want to see success in the lives that we are ministering to. As I share with you Leah's story, I am amazed at how God can use my insignificant life to significantly impact hers. Ultimately, though, her success story is really God's success story. I thankfully share in this because God has used me in some small way, but I must always remember the source and the power of this success.

As I experienced failure in my first two years of ministry, I realized that this really wasn't failure at all. God used that time to humble me and show me what success was really all about. As I pursued him in my life, I was changed. Because of this, my failure was really a success. It served to help me grow as a disciple of Christ and prepared me to be more effective in this ministry that he called me to.

As you pursue success in youth ministry, pursue God. Don't beat yourself up over those that don't respond. Be faithful to him in your life and in your ministry, and he will change the lives of your students. And as you pursue him, success happens; not just in your ministry life, but also in your personal life. Ultimately, he is the one that changes lives . . . even yours.

lemonade lessons

1. How successful is your ministry?

2. What criteria do you use to determine that success?

3. Is God significantly working and moving in your own life through your relationship with him?

4. What are you relying on to successfully change lives . . . your gifts, talents, and programs or God powerfully working in the hearts of your students?

5. Are there students that you just need to pray for? Take the time right now to lift them up to the Lord.

Paul Armitage

Paul has been in youth ministry for ten years. He enjoys speaking to students and parents at various retreats, camps, and youth events. When he's not celebrating Canadian holidays, playing Monopoly, grilling out, or traveling, he's spending time with his wife, Mandy and their two boys, Logan and Landon. They reside in Warren, Ohio, where Paul is the Youth Pastor at North-Mar Church.

To contact Paul:
parmitage@northmarchurch.com

from plexi-glass to tube socks . . . and i'm not talking indoor soccer

(restoring credibility after offending others)

I'm basically a dog person. I certainly, though, wouldn't want to offend my constituents who are cat people, and I should say that being, I hope, a sensitive person, that I have nothing against cats, and had cats when I was a boy, and if we didn't have the two dogs might very well be interested in having a cat now.[10]

—Congressman Jim Talent
(responding to the question: are you a dog or cat person?)

Periodically, any youth worker that has a pulse will have one of those BAD MINISTRY MOMENTS. It's when you have all the details planned out and everything is aligned for God to move, but something happens and what was once imagined as a night of close encounters with God ends up being a disaster (at least from your perspective).

There are many nights when I feel like I have conquered the world for Jesus. Everything . . . and I mean *everything*—from sound equipment, worship, teaching, to having serious life altering conversations with students comes off without a hitch. I'd debrief the night with several of our youth workers, and then re-live the sweet ministry moments again with my wife when I got home. These moments are what I live for. It's why you and I do youth ministry. It's what you and I were created to do.

Suddenly the alarm goes off and you wake up from dreamland when that parent walks (sometimes stomps) into your office the next day. You probably know what I mean, and if you don't—you will. He's so ticked off over something that took place the night before in youth group. Actually, he's more than just ticked, he's enraged, and a fleeting thought races across your mind . . . this could be the last meeting with a parent at this church that you'll ever have not because of the elder board, but because of the colt-45 he's hiding in his jacket. You can tell by the look on this parent's face that he is not all that excited about your "awesome" game that was played the night before. You know what I am talking about. But, if not, I've set the stage for you. Now let me share a couple of stories that involve "ticked off" parents and a naïve youth pastor.

I had only been youth pastor at the church for five weeks. It was a Wednesday night and the auditorium where the students met was frenzied and filled with anticipation. Just like any youth worker, I'm constantly thinking of games, activities, and experiences that will keep the attention of even the most apathetic students. On this one night, I had planned to do an outrageous game that involved plexi-glass and chocolate frosting. I absolutely knew that this game would be a "home run." No Doubt. The quickly raised hands resembled the audience wave at Fenway Park as I called for people to participate in this totally cool new game. I randomly picked two volunteers (or victims, depending on who you ask). As the students eagerly came forward, chocolate frosting was being smeared all over both sides of the plexi-glass. That's right . . . both sides had chocolate frosting caked on the surface.

As the plexi-glass was being held for the students, they began the competition to see who could lick their side the cleanest. As the students licked, the atmosphere had become electric as the entire group was cheering on both participants to lick like never before. The game was such a success, I decided to make it a tournament that would build on itself from week to week. So, for the following two weeks, sheets of plexi-glass were coated with chocolate frosting and the students licked away (all for the love of chocolate).

It was the final week of the plexi-glass tournament and the pandemonium had built to an all-time high. The tournament had boiled down to two students: a guy and a girl. This was the final round, and the grand-prize would be a free piece of plexi-glass and a half-used jar of chocolate frosting. There was a thrill in the air as the two contestants started licking the frosting from the plexi-glass. If it weren't for a thin piece of plastic, they would've been licking each other. It looked somewhat odd from my vantage point; but hey, students were laughing and having fun. They were engaged (not literally, of course—it might not have been so offensive if they really were "engaged"). Their tongues continued to clean the plexi-glass at speeds I didn't know the human tongue could lick. Finally, there was a winner. Everyone cheered. Students went home. I cleaned up. I thought the night was a complete success as students really had a great time until . . . a parent asked to see me the following morning at the church office.

Before I share my interaction with this parent and his interpretation of my lick-the-frosting-off-the-plexi-glass game, let me share with you one other activity that I botched—within a month of the plexi-glass game. Imagine with me: I had only been at this church for about ten weeks and was "in charge" of a junior high retreat. The TV show *Fear Factor* was just coming out, so all of our activities had a "fear factor" theme. One of our male leaders had planned all the games and activities, but it was one game that would be talked about for months to come. This game was simple because the only item needed was one white tube sock. This wasn't any run-of-the-mill tube sock. This tube sock had been used and reused without ever being washed. To help prepare for this specific game, an adult ran with the sock on for two weeks prior to the retreat. Following his morning jog, he gently placed the sock in a Ziploc® bag and sealed it shut. He repeated this seven or eight times with the same sock (without washing the sock), and periodically added a couple other delicacies like vinegar and orange juice. To say the least, the sock had a horrific smell that could easily be compared to a recently fertilized flower garden, or a guys' cabin on a junior high retreat. If tested under a microscope, one would have been able to find many microorganisms—some probably never previously identified. It was disgusting, but it fit into the master plan and would play a key part in the competition between teams.

The game was actually way too simple. Students were to elect a representative from their team to lower the sock into his or her mouth. After it was in this person's mouth, he or she had to keep it in for ten seconds. Once the sock was in, every person with a heartbeat (even the microorganisms) was shouting "1, 2, 3, 4 . . . " as loud as they could. Students were so grossed out, but they never looked back as they accepted the challenge to partake of the rotting, mildew infested, moldy tube sock. After administering IVs of Penicillin to every student who completed the task, points were added to their team's overall score. Chalk one up for the creative genius of this humble youth pastor and all those involved. In my book, it was a success since students were fully engaged and tapped into the spirit of the moment, until . . . now we get to the good part!

> From the tone of the letter, it was clear that they had lost any trust in me as a youth pastor, and the integrity of my ministry had been jeopardized.

It was the Monday following our retreat, and I was handed a three-page, single spaced letter from a mom and dad whose student attended the retreat. The letter didn't begin with a cordial greeting like I thought it would; rather, these parents were thoroughly disgusted with "one of the games" on the retreat. They communicated this to me loud and clear. The letter consisted of five or six reasons why this game was inappropriate and unsanitary for junior high students. From the tone of the letter, it was clear that they had lost any trust in me as a youth pastor, and the integrity of my ministry had been jeopardized. I felt like a complete failure. I felt unfairly attacked by these parents when, in my mind, I thought some significant spiritual milestones took place on our junior high retreat. How could I redeem myself as a youth pastor? How could I restore credibility to my ministry? These were questions that bombarded my thinking.

Remember the plexi-glass game? Well, there is an ending to that story as well. It was a Thursday morning, and one of the secretaries paged me and told me there was a parent that wanted to see me. As this father and I were walking together to sit down, I really did believe that he was there to tell me how his daughter was enjoying my ministry and connecting with other students. I was expecting encouragement and affirmation, but little did I know that I would be kicked and chastised for my irrehensible actions the prior evening. We sat down and I listened as he assaulted my creative genius with the plexi-glass game. He was disgusted with the game and told me that it had no place in a youth group setting. He told me that his daughter was watching a guy and a girl "go at it" right in front of everyone. He wanted me to know that his daughter's innocence was taken and that his trust in me as a man and a youth leader was minimized. This father finished our conversation by saying, "If this is what goes on in our youth ministry, my daughter will no longer be permitted to attend." Pseudo "French kissing" in the name of chocolate frosting lathered on a sheet of plexi-glass was, according to him, indicative of unwise, immature, and just plain bad leadership. I heard from this parent LOUD and CLEAR. I felt assaulted and criticized in my attempt to reach teenagers for Jesus.

No one likes to be attacked. Our human nature craves to be affirmed, built up, and complimented. Anytime someone comes along and accuses us (even if that

> I felt assaulted and criticized in my attempt to reach teenagers for Jesus.

accusation is filled with truth), our defenses go up and we're ready to fight back. I have learned through the above instances, and countless other times, that part of my job as a youth worker is keeping parents on my team; not ostracizing them. Although I haven't always followed this in my ministry, I've learned that youth ministry is easier when you *work* with parents instead of *fighting* with them. When trust in, and the integrity of, your ministry is compromised, it is hard to gain it back . . . but it's possible. If you're like me and you've lost the trust of a parent, keep reading. Enough with these stories! Now let's talk leadership, and the lessons that you and I can learn from a parent who's ticked off. Ready. Set. Let's Fight . . . I mean, Let's Roll.

Any person who's been in youth ministry for a long time will tell you that parents have the potential of being your greatest asset in youth ministry. As youth workers, we need to be relentless in keeping parents on our team. You probably have your own "plexi-glass and tube sock" stories, but for me, I've learned three invaluable lessons about how to stay connected with parents and watch them cheer me on from the sidelines.

the buck stops with parents

I've met youth workers who have an egotistical approach to youth ministry. They believe their way is the best way, and that any other way is nonsensical. When conflict occurs with a parent, this type of youth worker immediately puts up a wall and alienates the parent. This is not good. In fact, this attitude over time will undermine a youth worker's credibility and potentially destroy his or her ministry.

In the "plexi-glass and tube sock" examples, I was faced with a dilemma. Would I stick to my guns and alienate these disgruntled parents, or would I listen to their concerns and try to identify with their perspectives? From my mistakes in dealing with parents, I've learned that listening to parents and seeing things from their point of view helps to keep them on my team and directly impacts my effectiveness as a youth worker. Many youth workers believe that "the buck stops with them," but let's get real. The ones that really pull the strings are the parents; so, more accurately, the "buck stops with parents." If parents don't demonstrate confidence in a youth pastor, or youth worker, the lack of confidence will ultimately trickle down to the ministry and its programs. The end result: parents pulling the plug on their student attending any events. This would be detrimental and would prevent those students from experiencing community with other teenagers.

I am not suggesting that we become like a bunch of ants and get walked all over by parents. This is not leadership. There are instances when parents' grumbling or complaints are not valid. Our calling, I believe, is to be gracious, but not cave in to unrealistic demands and expectations. Most of the time though, parents really do want the best for their teenagers. The fact that they are concerned enough to come to you with an issue, or complaint, is indicative of the fact that they love their kid. In my experience, it has been the rare parent who wants to beat up and pummel the youth worker. Most parents do not want to beat you to a pulp; they just love their kids. So, before you react, remember that "the buck stops with parents." Listen to their concerns. Digest them. Look at things from their perspective...and whatever you do, work hard at keeping them on your team.

be a co-nurturer . . . not an event planner

Youth workers have become the quintessential event planners. Some of the greatest event planners I know are youth workers. They know how to throw a party. Give a youth worker a ten-dollar bill, an empty room, and thirty high school students, and you'll have an event that will blow away any college football tailgate party. In the midst of planning events, have we lost sight of one of our primary roles? We need to be nurturers; actually, co-nurturers with parents. Last time I checked, parents were the primary spiritual directors of their kids (Ephesians 6, Deuteronomy 6). A youth worker exists to help parents in the role they have as spiritual nurturers. We are to pray for students. Love them. Care for them. Teach them. Email them. Hang out with them.

> . . . parents have the potential of being your greatest asset in youth ministry.

When a parent sees a youth worker as a co-nurturer and not just an event planner, trust and credibility will instantly be given to your ministry. Parents will "buy in" to you and your ministry when they see you spending time and energy on their family. Our calling is to support, not cripple. Our job is to encourage parents, not overwhelm them. Our role is to walk beside parents, not desert them. We should be standing in parents' corner, urging them to be the parents that God has called them to be. It is one of the greatest ways we can invest our time. If you become one who nurtures, parents will be your biggest advocates, and they'll love you for it.

staying in relationship trumps being right

Most youth workers are mavericks. We're rebels. We love challenges. because we love to prove ourselves. In proving ourselves and proving the success of the ministry we work so hard to create, it is difficult for us to be confronted. When being confronted, we fight back. Fists cocked and gloves on, we want to pummel someone six feet under, especially if they have attacked a method or our ministry.

In the egotistical world that we live in, where people live and die for their rights, we need to willingly let go of the need to "be right." Being right is not as important as respecting someone else and staying in a relationship with him or her. Even if we're right and a parent is wrong, being in a relationship with that parent is more important than winning a verbal battle over a method. Parents are our biggest allies. I'm convinced of this. They can advance and catapult youth ministries to a higher level of achievement if they are on the same side as the youth worker. Leonard Sweet said: "Jesus saved the world by teaching twelve partners how to be family—how to get along together and belong to one another."[11] Our calling and biblical mandate is to "get along" with parents. Give up your right to be right. Relationship trumps being right. So let me say this: honor, listen, and love the parents in your youth

> Jesus saved the world by teaching twelve partners how to be family—how to get along together and belong to one another.
>
> —Leonard Sweet
> theologian, author, futurist

ministry. The Apostle Paul summed it up pretty well in Philippians 2:3, "but in humility, consider others better than yourselves." This is not easy stuff. Getting along with parents is a daily challenge we must embrace if we are to ensure our ministry receives respect from the "parentals."

Remember that parent who was "ticked off" at the tube sock game? He became a great supporter and later served in our junior high ministry, led a small group, and even taught at some of our evening sessions. His trust in me was restored . . . but it started with attitude. I had to disarm my defensiveness and listen to him as a concerned parent. I'm grateful I did. Youth ministry is more fun and more exciting when parents work *with you* and not *against you*. It takes discipline, humility, and hard work to keep parents on your team . . . but it is worth all the blood and sweat (and sometimes tears). Working with parents and keeping them on your side makes life and ministry easier. So, work with the parents in your youth ministry. Respect them. Love them. Be humble in front of them. If you do, they will back you up and follow you as a leader. Trust me, I know from experience.

lemonade lessons

1. What "Plexi-glass or tube sock" story do you have that is fresh in your mind? How did you navigate yourself and others through the conflict? Were you able to resolve the conflict with parents and bring them back on your team? How can you handle things differently in the future?

2. Are parents and/or adults scared of you? Intimidated by you? Why? If parents or other adults find you unapproachable, how can you change your demeanor, your attitude, or your reactions? Do you handle constructive criticism well?

3. How can you be a better co-nurturer to parents in your church or organization? What are some things you can do that would allow parents to have a deeper trust in you as a youth worker? When was the last time you hand wrote a letter to a parent expressing your appreciation to him or her (if not lately, maybe this week would be a good time)?

4. Do you listen to parents in your ministry? Is there a "forum" or "vehicle" in place where parents can voice concerns (and affirmations)? Do you have a ministry that invites feedback from parents? Do parents in your church feel invited? Feel wanted?

Andrew Bonaventura

Lemonade maker Andrew Bonaventura is an experienced youth pastor, gifted communicator, writer, and loving husband and father. He loves investing in others and being very active in ministry balanced with plenty of good time for living from the heart with family and friends. Ministry areas of great interest to him are leadership development, inspiring teaching, creative thinking, and coaching/mentoring. Andrew enjoys listening to live and recorded music, Dunkin' Donuts coffee, working out, fishing, traveling, and being in the outdoors. However, he most enjoys being married to Christine and shepherding his two great sons! Andrew is an ordained pastor, native of New Jersey, cum laude graduate of Houghton College, and speaks or teaches regularly to many different groups of people in ministry settings.

Andrew is available for ministry consultation, speaking, and training.

To contact Andrew:
andrewbonaventura@gmail.com

lemon 6

when innovations don't get standing ovations

(making changes the wrong way)

Great innovations should not be forced on slender majorities.

—Thomas Jefferson

thought everyone would love the changes I creatively came up with for
the high school ministry in transition time. Everyone—leaders on the
team, students, parents—was going to heave a sigh of relief once they
learned of the innovations I'd be introducing, or so I expected. But these
innovations would receive no standing ovation, and I had a lot to learn
about how to think through and introduce change, especially in relation
to how a team processes it. This is the story of a youth pastor who got
too far ahead of himself, his valued team members, and probably God in
the excited pursuit of change. Changes intended to be for the good of
many, but which instead turned out to be for the frustration of many.
God was certainly gracious enough to teach me some great life lessons
about leadership, team-building, and the importance of process, but not
without having to learn them the hard way. Let me take you through my
story and share how this leadership mistake shaped my life and ministry.

my story

I was the middle school pastor in a large, growing church in southwest New Jersey for about three years, doing well and very much enjoying the work God had for me. As middle school pastor, I worked closely with our church's high school pastor those three years and had a lot of connection with students who moved from eighth grade into high school, as well as with leaders in the high school ministry. Overall, the youth ministry in our church was very positive, well-oiled, and fairly cohesive across the middle school/high school ministry divide. Change was on the horizon though.

In my third year ministering as middle school pastor the high school pastor transitioned out of youth ministry (after nine years in it at our church) into another ministry role, still remaining on staff at the same church. Higher leadership in our church met with me and cast a very encouraging vote of confidence, asking if I'd consider serving as pastor over all the church's youth ministries. This would include keeping the middle school ministry running well, helping the high school ministry operate smoothly through the staff transition time, casting future vision for the youth ministry overall, building the youth ministry department staff team by making some hires, and more. After seriously praying and thinking this offer through with my wife and others for about a month, I was assured the Lord was calling me to this next level of ministry responsibility, personal stretching, and spiritual challenge. I accepted the promotion and immediately began praying, thinking, planning, and writing all sorts of ideas that came to mind.

So here began the mistake. I was somehow convinced in my own mind that coming up with new ways to do things, creative changes, and other innovations would be what everyone was hoping for. Problem was

> Only man is not content to leave things as they are, but must always be changing them, and when he has done so, is seldom satisfied with the result.
>
> —Elspeth Huxley
> celebrated writer &
> political thinker

I really didn't include veterans—good, faithful ones who were serving in the high school ministry with great fruit—in processing the changes. On the other hand, you wouldn't find me off on my own hatching ideas privately, but I certainly did not lean on the collective strength of others in this transition time. Complicating matters a bit further for me, higher leadership saw this transition time as an opportunity to implement their ideas for change. I probably had a desire to please them and at the same time be a hero-savior for the big youth ministry in a state of flux. I also lacked good communication to keep the team well-prepared and with me. Furthermore, I was getting caught up in minor nonessential program tweaks (like meeting space décor, for instance), on a sort of "let's just change all the things we've always talked about" kick.

Let me share an example to put some flesh on what it was like for others living with my innovation frenzy at the time. One of the changes higher leadership wanted me to implement was to double the schedule of the regular high school large group gathering. In our church the high school ministry historically operated on an alternating Monday night schedule of large group, small group, large group, small group. The plan was to get the large group meeting every Monday night and small groups meeting on another day that could be freely chosen by the students and leaders in a group together. If you're picking up on the story, you're probably asking what in the world I was thinking leading a large youth ministry in a transition time without enough staff and essentially doubling the work load for all. I recall one leader in an exasperated moment who exclaimed something like, "I feel like we're in war, we've lost some men, and are now marching into battles we shouldn't be!"

Over the next several months I tuned in to what my leaders, students, and others were saying about both the type and pace of changes being posed. When I'd take more frequent steps back into reality, it became quite clear that I didn't have to champion so much change so quickly. We were all in a transition time together, and that called for circling the wagons and preserving some energy for the road ahead. Furthermore, I was learning how humility (not pride) would pave the way for us all to achieve progress. Was I ever mistaken about introducing change! Now I know, and want to share with you, that changes can be more successfully introduced by learning and practicing several key team-building principles.

understanding my mistakes

"Those who cannot remember the past are condemned to repeat it," warned George Santayana. The mistake I just retold is certainly one I've learned a great lesson from, and I try hard not to repeat it. This mistake not only was the source of a frustrating and somewhat painful lesson, but also had the opposite effect I was hoping my actions would produce in the first place. When I recall the many ripples coming from this mistake, I can't believe that I actually thought I knew what I was doing then!

> Pride goes before destruction, and a haughty spirit before a fall.
>
> – Proverbs 16:1

First, and probably most glaring to me as I look back, was my *pride getting in the way of everything.* I mentioned earlier my desire to be the rescue hero for the youth ministry in such a stretching transition time, kind of like visions of sugar plums dancing in my head. There were a lot of needs at that time requiring action, but I don't know why I believed that I could be the one person providing for all those needs. Arrogance wasn't so much the issue here as was underlying self-centered thinking that made me try to figure out things on my own. I think I wanted to come up with great solutions, present these solutions to those involved in the ministry, and feel good about providing answers for people. Deep in my heart there likely existed a motive of helping others, but it came out as the desire to be recognized as a wonderful answer man given by God to this ministry. Man, does pride stink when you stop and take a whiff!

Second, I was stricken with the fever of *innovation just for innovation's sake.* I'm the kind of person who remembers all sorts of ideas, details, and desires once talked about. Combine this with the power to put these once-talked-about-things in motion, and you've got a lot of changes taking place that probably shouldn't have had energy thrown at them. You may be familiar with the saying about leaders who rearrange the deck chairs on the Titanic; that could have nicely applied here. In one breath I was suggesting significant changes, like an alternate approach to our youth staff model, while at the same time brainstorming new ways to have game stations available for kids as they arrived for our program. In some cases I was wrapped up in several changes just because it was a change! As I look back it appears I was like a kid in a candy shop who bought and ate too much only to find himself sick shortly thereafter. An innovation frenzy like this is frustrating to people you lead because they don't need (or necessarily like) to have that many new ideas thrown at them at one time. People cannot easily assimilate volumes of change all at once, especially if changes have little rhyme or reason.

Another component of my mistake I've come to understand was my *lack of reliance upon collective advice and wisdom.* I neglected the skill of including others in the process of decision making for proposed changes. The truth that all of us are a lot smarter than any one of us alone was overlooked. While I should have regarded team members as partners, they were, in my mind, more like an audience to wow and please. When I made changes and didn't take the time to run them by others, seek their feedback, and operate by a listening ear, I wound up losing the support and direction I actually sought. One example I recall was trying to reinvent and rename the high school small group program from 'Breakaway' to 'ReaLife' without including many leaders of those groups at all in the process. My team was in the trenches doing youth ministry routinely with high schoolers while I was a 'recent import' to their world. How good it would have been to ask these very devoted members what possible changes were most needed and start with ideas arising from their experience and collective wisdom. By not seeking enough advice from my ministry veterans, I spent a lot of energy on endeavors that probably were not welcome changes, let alone immediately helpful ones.

Lastly, my mistake was accentuated by poor *communication with my team members* about where things were heading. Picture this: a large youth ministry in a big transition, devoted leaders wanting to know what the future holds, a

> The art of communication is the language of leadership.
>
> – James Humes
> Royals Professor Of
> Language & Leadership

mistaken leader making too many changes too quickly . . . and now add to the mix skimpy organizational communication from the one who should be the communicator! I probably suffered from the combination of not knowing exactly what to communicate and simply not prioritizing team communication in my weekly use of time. The result was that my team was frustrated, confused, and unable to function in unity.

avoiding my mistake in the future

The mistake of changing too many things too fast for too many is one I pray I'm not likely to repeat, but wishful thinking won't help me avoid it. Winston Churchill cautioned, "All men make mistakes, but only wise men learn from their mistakes." Through my mistake I have gained new understanding of healthy ways to implement change. What follows is some advice based on my own reflection for how the different aspects of my mistake can be quite easily avoided in the future.

First, *check your personal pride,* ego, or whatever you want to call it. Having confidence placed in you and possessing power doesn't automatically mean that all will look to you for answers. Abandon the self-centered approach to ministry leadership where you find yourself believing the whole thing rests on your shoulders. I believe much of my mistake stemmed from this root issue because it blinded me from the true, real needs of others existent at the time. It has been said that swallowing your pride seldom leads to indigestion, so have no fear of taking a big step back to see things outside of your own perspective. Be confident in your God-given calling, but always do so with genuine humility.

> Swallowing your pride seldom leads to indigestion.
>
> – Anonymous

Second, *focus on the most important things,* not the peripheral possibilities. For instance, I was worrying about how the cool, new party lights would look in our big outdoor gathering tent while up front I've got a guy leading worship bare-chested! Just because you can think of a change to make doesn't mean it is important to make or that it requires your time and energy. My time and energy would have been better spent developing this student worship leader a bit more. If I had done a better job of discussing matters with my team, the essential changes would have been obvious instead of obscured. Don't get carried away with creative opportunities when you haven't done your homework on the essentials needed most in your current situation.

Third, *leaders have followers, teams, and supporters—treat these people lovingly, trust them greatly, and listen to them attentively.* Including, relying on, and building with others is how virtually all good things in history have been accomplished. There's nothing wrong with thinking things through on your own, developing good ideas in your own mind, and being convinced that your ideas can add value to endeavors. However, neglecting to share those ideas with your team (your valued community of people) will not only portray you as an island, but cause you to miss out on important idea-refinement, learning, personal growth, and better progress. When leading a team through changes, rely on the team.

Finally, when leading others through change, *exercise productive communication* that both informs and encourages. One of the ways I began rebuilding trust with my team was by sending a weekly email to everyone. This routine communication piece started with a personal paragraph of encouragement to my team, followed by several informational updates (how the search for

> Communication is depositing a part of yourself in another person.
>
> – Anonymous

another staff member was going, church-wide developments, etc.), followed by a bullet list of upcoming youth ministry dates and events. Several times I heard through the grapevine that this is exactly what team members wanted and needed. However you decide to do it, your conscientious communication, especially in times of change, will help flourish others instead of frustrate them.

God uses mistakes

Making this mistake ended up being a truly beneficial lesson for me. I'm not saying I'm glad for the grit it took me through, but I am glad for how God spoke to my heart and led me so well. Of great encouragement to me at the time was an article I read in Campus Crusade for Christ's magazine, *Worldwide Challenge*, back in May-June 2003. Steve Douglass, now president of Campus Crusade, shared in an article entitled, "Helping Heroes," how he sought God for what the grand strategy should be for this worldwide ministry as he would become the next president after Bill Bright. Steve beautifully explained how such a large and diverse ministry as Campus Crusade could not be effectively led by one strategy, but that "many strong leaders and other staff members could individually receive specific strategies from God . . . ." He went on to say, "Instead of having to announce some dramatic new 'secret to success,' I could simply look my fellow staff members in the eye and explain that they represented the key to the ministry's future. God was going to place into their minds and hearts the 'breakthrough' new ideas that would throw open the doors to increased ministry effectiveness. They were the heroes, and my job was to help them."

When you are the leader of a group and are considering changes or introducing innovation, save yourself (and others) both the headache and heartache that comes from changing too much, too fast, for too many. Good leaders pay attention to process, particularly during times of change. May you figure out with God and others how to avoid making my mistake in your own context and take the productive path of implementing change.

lemonade lessons

1. After reading this chapter on implementing change, what changes are you considering in ministry? Are they truly essential? Are there any non-essential changes you are considering? Is there a "best" time to implement changes?

2. What are some methods you can implement?

3. What role does pride play in your decision-making for your ministry? How might your ministry be hindered by pride?

4. Overall, what do you feel God is saying to you most clearly through this chapter? Choose a trusted ministry friend with whom to share this and make any necessary personal course correction.

John Byrne

John has been involved in youth ministry for more then 13 years. His ability to engage, challenge, and speak relevantly to his audience has led to speaking opportunities nationwide including camps, seminars, conferences, and training events. He has also been published in Group Magazine and was part of the writing team for Connexion, an interactive student evangelism and Biblical worldview experience.

John knew he wanted to be a youth pastor at the early age of 13. While attending Oak Hills Bible College, he met the woman of his dreams and convinced her to marry him. After a two year honeymoon in Colorado, he returned to Minnesota to finish his Biblical Studies degree from Northwestern Bible College.

John's passion is living out the Great Commission in his life and helping others do the same. He does this through writing and speaking, as well as missional living in his own neighborhood and community.

John is currently the Lead Pastor of Water's Edge Church (www.wechurch.com), a church plant in Blaine, Minnesota. He works with youth at camps and conferences as much as his schedule allows. He lives in Ham Lake, Minnesota, with his wife Christa, daughter Catrina (age 7), and son Joash (age 1).

To contact John:
pj@pjs-web.net
www.pjs-web.net
763.222.9907

if I had only been known

(leading through biblical community)

I accepted my first youth ministry position at the age of seventeen. Sounds crazy, but there were kids in the youth group who were almost a year older than me I was. The $79 a month I was paid did little more than pay for gas. Believe it or not, this was not the 60's or even the 70's. It was the early 90's, and I jumped into ministry with both feet. I loved God and loved students. I thought that was enough. I knew God had changed my life, and I was hoping He would use me as He changed the lives of others.

Being a pastor is almost par for the course in my family. My grandpa is a pastor, and my uncle is a pastor. Growing up I heard stories of what ministry is like, both good and bad. Even in college I heard how hard ministry is. I felt the pressure before I even started. Paul warned Timo-

> The saying is trustworthy: If anyone aspires to the office of overseer, he desires a noble task.
>
> – 1 Timothy 3:1

thy about the importance of leadership roles in the church. Leadership requires much of a person's character. To this day I get a little scared when I read 1 Timothy 3. This intimidating list of qualifications can make even spiritual giants quiver in their boots. Of course, I no longer believe in spiritual giants.

I have come to realize even the "spiritual giants" we find in scripture had some serious chinks in their armor. I wondered what people would think if they knew I didn't have it all together or how much being "spiritual" was a struggle for me. What if someone knew how many times I missed devotions or how little I prayed last week? What if someone heard about me yelling at the umpire for calling me out? What if someone knew about my sin? There seems to be an inherent pressure to have it all together for those who are in ministry.

having it all together

My mom told me those in leadership live in glass houses. Glass houses are fragile and transparent. When I began ministry and moved into my glass house, the first thing I did was tint the glass.

Allowing people to become close was simply not an option. Allowing people to know me intimately would only set me up to be hurt and probably to fail. I always thought I should have a good friend outside of my ministry. A friend I could be honest with, trust, and someone I could share struggles with. That wasn't a bad idea, but it wasn't enough.

Maybe it was my own fault, but I believed I couldn't struggle with anything if I was going to be in leadership. I thought I had to be righteous, holy, and sinless. While it may be unintentional, some churches have created a culture of false integrity. They have created a culture where it is difficult to live an authentic Christian life because law is emphasized over grace and biblical community. Over and over again the Sermon on the Mount or some other scripture is used like a cat of nine tails to punish all of those who dare admit they struggle with sin or don't live up to the standards of what it means to be "spiritual."

I have watched as pastors and youth pastors have lost their jobs because of moral indiscretions, and it seems like every time those around them are taken back by the moral failure. They are surprised that such a "Godly person" could do such a terrible thing. I might suggest that failure to live in biblical community is what allows those in leadership to go down a path that leads to moral failure.

The consequences of living this way are significant and long term. Not only will this lead to a lack of authentic community for you, but also your family and your ministry.

pressure on the family

My wife, Christa, and I have been doing ministry together since before we were even dating. I don't want to get all sentimental, but she gives me confidence. I know even if I really mess up, she will be there for me.

I use to put a lot of pressure on her to keep quiet about the things we struggled with in our marriage. I was scared of what people might think. In an effort to keep my reputation in tact, I kept her from having healthy relationships where she could be honest about the things she was struggling with. What a horrible way to live. This is not a godly way to treat your spouse.

Whether this kind of pressure is real or perceived, it is the kind of pressure that can destroy a family. At the very least, it will cause the relationships in the family to become unhealthy. At worst, it could drive a wedge between husband and wife, causing one or both to break.

reaching the breaking point

My dad always told me to buy Craftsman tools. These tools are made tough. Sears is so confident in their tools, that they offer a lifetime warranty. If you break one of their tools, they will replace it—no questions asked. On one occasion my brother and I were taking the hub off my car.

> Then Jesus said, "Come to me, all of you who are weary and carry heavy burdens, and I will give you rest. Take my yoke upon you. Let me teach you, because I am humble and gentle, and you will find rest for your souls. For my yoke fits perfectly, and the burden I give you is light."
>
> – Matthew 11:20-30 (NLT)

We were using a Craftsman breaker bar to loosen the nut. We made four trips to Sears that day. Sears replaced the breaker bar without question every time.

The lesson I learned was this: if you apply enough pressure to anything, it will break. This is true with tools, and it is true with people.

Eventually I reached a point where I wanted so desperately for someone to know me, but I was scared. I wanted to be what I was pretending to be. Jesus promised to be our rest. He promised his yoke would be light, but the yoke I carried was not the yoke Jesus promised. It was something more.

I never did develop enough guts to seek the kind of authentic community I knew I needed. Eventually, I was confronted about some areas of my life. I was so relieved, I could hardly contain myself. It was difficult, but I could finally be honest with someone. Not long after that I was invited to participate with a small group of guys in holding each other accountable for all kinds of things—spiritual, moral, family, and more. These men, in some sense, became Jesus to me. I began to feel the yoke of Jesus. Allowing myself to be vulnerable with these men was risky, but it paid off.

risking everything

Several years ago while on vacation with my family in Steamboat, Colorado, my wife *allowed* me to go back country skiing for a day. I loved almost every second of it. Skiing is amazing, but skiing powder, waist deep, all day long is almost beyond description. I had the opportunity to ski off cliffs and jump off snow covered rocks. On the last run of the day, I decided to show off a little bit. I jumped off a huge rock and attempted a helli (I turned 360 degrees in the air). Unfortunately, I over rotated. When I hit the ground, I was sideways. One ski came off and the other didn't. I spent the next morning in the hospital being told I would need surgery on my knee. Still, I wouldn't give back that day for anything.

Making the choice to be involved in authentic community is risky. If you have been in ministry for very long, you have heard about some youth worker being let go because the games being played were too gross, he wanted to paint the walls too brightly, or some other crazy reason. Maybe it happened to you. Imagine what might happen if a few people in your congregation found out how much you struggle with your prayer life. Worse, what would happen if someone found out you struggle with lust, or you have doubts about God?

I'm not generally scared of breaking some bones or tearing up my body, but I have been scared of losing my job or hurting my reputation because someone knew my struggles. That kind of risk is different.

You may have everything to lose, but you have everything to gain as well. Not long ago we had a couple visit our church for the first time. They immediately recognized some people they knew. Because of the teacher-student relationship between these people outside the church, they decided not to come back. They made this choice not because the relationship was bad, but because they didn't feel they could participate in our community the way they wanted to. In other words, they didn't want to risk being authentic. Everyone lost out in that situation. They missed an opportunity to have great impact on some students in our church, and our students missed the opportunity to watch someone live there faith in and out of the church.

> Restlessness and discontent are the first necessities of progress.
>
> – Thomas Edison
> inventor & entrepreneur extraordinaire

I have risked everything and gained everything. I now have friends in my church that will challenge me and encourage me. They will listen to my struggles and withhold judgment. I will do the same thing for them.

I sometimes wonder what would have happened to David if it hadn't been for Nathan, or what if Moses didn't have Jethro? David suffered for his sin, but he was restored in part thanks to Nathan. Moses was trying to do everything, but his burden was lightened because Jethro was there to help him think things through. Both David and Moses would have been miserable without the people around them being involved in their lives.

finding biblical community

Over and over again we hear the importance of developing a loving atmosphere and culture within our ministries. We know if someone attends a program or event and does not connect with someone, they will probably not return. The result of this kind of teaching is that we have become very good at training greeters and even following up with post cards and phone calls. Many ministries have created environments where people feel welcome, but this does not mean there is a culture of biblical community.

Biblical community flows out of the gospel itself. Christ came to earth to save us, expressing love in its purest form. When Paul speaks of love in 1 Corinthians 13, he speaks of a love that "does not rejoice in wrongdoing, but rejoices with truth" and "endures all things." This kind of love is not easily deterred. In Romans 12, Paul speaks of a community which encourages and even challenges the individual to honor God, hate evil, love good, and to serve the Lord. Biblical community does not demand perfection; it simply drives the imperfect to the cross. Biblical community understands that we cannot achieve righteousness; we can only receive the righteousness of Christ.

Finding this kind of community means seeking the kinds of relationships where honesty and authenticity are rewarded with more of the same. For me this meant developing relationships with four other guys who shared their deepest darkest secrets while knowing I would continue to love them. Two of the men in this group were elders in the church, and two of them served with me in youth ministry. I had to trust the judgment of these men, and they had to trust me.

The most dangerous and the best place to look for these relationships is among those in leadership over you and those who minister alongside you. If you want authenticity to be valued by those around you, they must see it in you. If you want them to live in biblical community, they need to see you live in biblical community.

Here are a few very simple and practical ideas for developing this kind of intimate community in your life:

Intentionally seek out relationships with a few people by spending time with them. Invite them to your house, go fishing with them, and just hang out with them.

When the time is right, *invite them to participate in a more intimate relationship.* Ask them to commit to pray for you, and you commit to pray for them.

Schedule regular times to get together. We would often get together after our wives and kids were in bed. This meant a late night once in a while, but it was worth it.

free to minister

One of the most difficult topics for me to preach or teach about is holiness or sanctification. It's hard because I know myself too well. I constantly find myself running to the foot of the cross because I need to be reminded of the blood that cleansed me. I realize that without the blood of Christ, I'm not even close to being holy or righteous. Whether I am teaching about abstinence, loving the unlovable, or making godly decisions, I realize that my righteousness does not come from obeying God's law, it comes from Christ.

This truth has revolutionized my ability to participate in biblical community and to minister to others. I don't have to be the perfect example. This truth makes it eas*ier* (not necessarily easy) to live in biblical community. I don't need to have it all together in order to preach, teach, or even worship.

When I realized that, even as a Christian, I was going to battle with my sin nature and needed to spend more time at the foot of the cross, I became more passionate about the gospel. I preach the gospel every week, not because I am trying to convert people, although that happens, but because Christians need to be reminded they still need the gospel message every day. Jesus did not only pay for my past sins, but my future sins as well. As a leader, I am no different. Integrity isn't only about doing what is right; it is about dealing with what is wrong.

free to lead

At one point after struggling with some sin, my wife asked me how I could lead worship. I don't remember what I said, but a person who realizes the necessity and importance of the blood of Christ is the best person to lead worship. At that time all I wanted to do was run to my Savior and thank him for the righteousness he had given me. Biblical community drives sinners, saved or unsaved, to the cross. The leader of this kind of community should be first in line, and if the leader runs to the cross, there will always be someone following. That is the most powerful kind of leadership anyone can have. I am free to lead because "it is for freedom that Christ has set me free" (Galatians 5). Christ did not die on the cross to impose the law on my life; he died to free me from the burden of the law. For this, I love my Jesus!!

When a leader is willing to look someone in the eye and tell him, "I messed up" or "I need help," the message being communicated is not only humility, but authenticity and the willingness to submit. When I began to live in authentic community, my ministry became more powerful. This didn't happen because I became more powerful, but because the gospel became more powerful.

I am free to lead because I no longer have to lead from a position of perfection or even power. Being authentic and living in biblical community is simply living beneath the cross. Jesus came not to heal the healthy and save the righteous, but to heal the sick and save the unrighteous. I, along with Paul, am a sinner; a sinner set free by the blood of Jesus. I am no longer condemned. I want to cry out with William Wallace: "F-R-E-E-D-O-M!"

lemonade lessons

1. What kinds of pressures have you felt from being in a position of leadership? Do you think those pressures are real or perceived?

2. What kinds of pressures should those in leadership feel?

3. How can living in biblical community keep those in leadership from major moral failures?

4. What does it mean to be free? What should the Christian be free from according to Galatians 5?

5. What scares you the most about being authentic and transparent?

6. How can you help those around you live in biblical community?

7. What are some things you can do to begin to create a culture where biblical community is highly valued? What roadblocks are in place right now?

Peter Doan

Peter was born in Los Angeles, California, lived in Hong Kong, went to school in Malaysia, is Vietnamese, and has traveled to many countries in Asia, Africa, Europe, and the North America. Raised as a missionary kid and pastor's kid, his diversity, both in his cultural experience and language abilities, has put him in an interesting ministry where cultures collide. He is a youth pastor at a Vietnamese Church in Orange County, California, where his students are English speaking, and their parents are Vietnamese speaking. He also takes on the role of administrative pastor with the English Speaking Vietnamese congregation at his church (a church within a church church-plant).

Peter's passions include leadership, organization, speaking, problem solving, training, and consulting. He is a frequent guest speaker at churches and camps across the United States. He does consultation for starting youth ministries as well as multi-ethnic ministries. As a musician, he leads worship at his church, at camps, and develops worship leaders.

Peter's education and interests are as diverse as his background. He graduated with a Bachelor of Arts in Music Liberal Arts, piano emphasis, and Biblical Studies at Simpson University in Redding, California. He continued his studies at Azusa Pacific University, and graduated with an M.Div with an emphasis in Youth Ministry and Worship Leadership. Peter enjoys an active life that includes mountain biking, snowboarding, weightlifting, reading, bowling, shooting pool, and traveling, especially traveling spontaneously. His interests are in technology, psychology, science, and history.

To contact Peter:
www.peterdoan.com

lemon 8

radar detector on the dashboard of life

(detecting life trials and learning from them)

Everything is permissible—but not everything is beneficial. Everything is permissible—but not everything is constructive. Nobody should seek his own good, but the good of others.

—The Apostle Paul

I discovered the art of online auctions when eBay first started. I had no idea what to buy. So, with my great wisdom and insight, I found something that I wanted to get.

I'll be perfectly honest. I love driving. I love driving fast. My favorite video games are racing simulators where the first one wins, and the winner does everything possible to reach that prize. So what did I end up getting on eBay? A radar detector!

I look back now and ask, "Why?" Well, for one, it was such a cool toy. And two, the feeling of winning was great. "I am the winner. You are the loser. Nah, nah, nah, nah, nah, nah. Ha, ha, ha, ha, ha, ha." Third, I love radar detectors! Mine would beep and tell me what kind of radar the highway patrol was using. I'd test it out at airports with those speed monitor things that tell you that you're going too fast. I think it even caught the signals from automatic doors at supermarkets. And finally, I could now drive fast, weave in and out of traffic, and not get caught.

I bought the radar detector a few months before I started leading the youth group at my first church. I didn't think much of it at the time. I actually slowed down a lot because the dumb thing kept going off. Like I said earlier, it would go off at almost anything. Most of the time the beeps were false alarms. Because of that, I drove the speed limit. But the day came when I got caught. Not by an officer, mind you, but by a student. I have no doubt that people in my church were already talking about it, but I realized my cirme when my student asked me, "Isn't it illegal to have a radar detector?" Of course, being defensive of the pride and joy of my first eBay win, I replied with, "No, it's legal." And of course, youth being youth, he asked me back, "Don't you speed when you have it on though? Isn't that breaking the law?" I was stumped. I couldn't respond. He was right.

After almost a decade of youth ministry, I learned something profound: youth work is difficult. Everyone's eyes are on you. Kids copy you, parents question you, and pastors don't always get what you do. If you're lucky, you have a supportive pastor who gives you the benefit of the doubt. But for the most part, you're expected to perform miracles in students' lives, give them good morals, have them get good grades, prevent them from being degenerates of society, maintain fun yet educational programming, and the list goes on. On top of that, parents expect you to have good character and a perfect life. "Sin" and "leader" never go together. No pressure! It's a tough task. When someone doesn't agree with you, or when students tell their parents about the "cool" thing you did at youth group that wasn't good or bad, but questionable, trouble comes. Sometimes they make a stink about it by spreading rumors or talking behind your back—bashing your ministry, your character, and your calling. If you're lucky, they'll confront you head on. Your heart is in question. You sense your credibility decreasing. You confidence is down. Some leave the ministry. Others go on feeling inadequate, never recovering and limping their way through ministry carrying baggage that may never be let go.

I have another story. Not too long ago, I was watching a video clip in my office. It was something that aired on MAD TV about ten years ago about the Terminator going back to Jesus' time to protect him. Sometimes when I speak, I refer to the "Simpson's" or other TV shows.

One kid in particular took note of that. He went home and, against his dad's rules, watched the "Simpson's." Dad comes home, sees him, and asks, "Why are you watching the Simpson's?" In his defense, he said I watch it and told his dad not to have a cow. Piqued with interest and fumed with anger, his dad asked, "What else do you guys do at church?" This kid listed all the things that, in my eyes, were just regular things—things that are biblically sound, theologically correct, but not traditionally acceptable. The Mad TV sketch about the Terminator going back to Jesus' time to protect him was the kicker. It was the last straw! Even though Jesus was in character, and it didn't really mess with Jesus (his deity or his character), the fact that it took Jesus and used him in a comedy sketch, to his dad, was appalling and broke the commandment of not taking God's name in vain. To make a long story short, I was called into a meeting. I had to explain myself, and then was told that if a leader were to cause a young child to stumble, he should throw himself off a cliff. I was also told that this father and his family probably won't be going to my church. I was deemed irresponsible, a blasphemer, and not worthy to be a youth pastor. Ouch! The whole youth ministry was in question and rumors were flying around with the parents and students asking questions to why this student was no longer going to church.

Even though my conscience was clear, the things I did caused someone to stumble and leave the church. As for the kid, his view of the Christian faith had come to a fork in the road. Was his dad right? Was his youth pastor right?

Sure, all things may be permissible, but just because we can do something, is it worth the price we have to pay in the long run? Is it worth having turmoil when that same energy could be focused somewhere else if only we had a little more discretion and thought things out more carefully? As leaders, we will be on the chopping block for a lot of things. We have to be sharp and think things through before we act. We have to evaluate current actions that are already in play. We need to have a radar detector on our dashboards of life and ministry.

the things we do ... the questionable things

Youth leaders have the most fun. I sometimes feel bad for people like my dad (who is a senior pastor) or my senior pastor who have to minister to adults. They don't seem to have as much fun as I do. But one thing youth leaders have to constantly figure out is where the line is drawn between "acceptable" and "unacceptable." The tricky part is when the line is so thin or faded, opinion is what defines it and nothing is clear.

Having a radar detector wasn't illegal or unbiblical. It was questionable. Okay ... fine, fine. Some of you would say it was down right wrong. But for me, I believe it actually helped me drive the speed limit. Still, it raised questions towards my character.

So how can we know what to do and what not to do? Is there a clear formula? There isn't anything really concrete except for the fact that we are to be above reproach (1 Timothy 3:2-3). But for me, there are a few things that I do. First, I ask myself, "Is it legal?" Seems like a dumb question, but in all actuality there are things that go on in our youth ministry that may be illegal. For example, six kids riding in a car made for five. Sometimes we even encourage that or look the other way. Sometimes video clips or movies are shown without proper authorization, or we photocopying something that was copyrighted. The list goes on. Sure, it seems dumb, but it's rudimentary and something that usually goes unchecked. How do we know if we're doing something illegal? Ask someone. Talk to people who work with you in the youth ministry, your pastor, some parents that you trust, or the church's insurance company.

The second thing to look out for is the church's cultural context. As youth leaders, we work mainly with two different cultures: the student culture and the parent culture. Paul talks about being all things to all people. In our ministry, we need to be able to understand our students' culture, but also understand their parents' particular culture and situation, and be able to minister to both.

Getting to know your students' culture isn't too hard. Go to their school and listen to their conversations with their friends. Be observant. You'll learn tons. Check out their blog sites or read up on current cultural trends from youth ministry magazines. Or do what I like to do— sit at a mall on a Saturday afternoon and just see what students are like, what they buy, how they act around other friends, what they wear, and what they value.

Getting to know the parents is a key element as well. Communication is very important. Beyond letting parents know events that are going on in the youth ministry, youth leaders need to spend time getting to know parents and praying for them. The youth pastor will be an ally of the parents if some sort of alliance has been made. Parents can be your biggest cheering squad or your most lethal firing squad. It all depends on how you communicate with them.

My example about the dad who confronted me could have been avoided if I spent more time talking to him and getting to know his family situation. He and his son don't talk to each other much. When his son disobeyed his dad and then used me as a get-out-of-jail-free card, in a sense, I underminded his authority over his son. If he knew me and the purposes of the youth ministry, he probably wouldn't have been so angry with me.

Getting to know your church and the church leadership is also crucial. A question you may want to ask the church leaders is: "What past issues were on trial relating to the youth ministry?" From there, an assessment can be made on what you plan to do and what you're currently doing. Spending some time conversing with your church leaders would yield understanding on both sides. You slowly know what the church's expectations are, and your credibility as a listener and learner builds over time. When tough times come, they are more likely to stand behind you because they know your heart. My senior pastor stood behind me when

I was confronted by this parent. It was such an encouragement knowing someone had my back during this hard time.

But in youth ministry, there will always be some controversial things that we do. Make sure you're willing to stand trial for it. Make sure your controversial things have a real purpose behind them, and that they really do accomplish those purposes. Log down all things. Being organized will save you in the long run. And most of all, COMMUNICATE, COMMUNICATE, COMMUNICATE. Let your superior know what you're doing.

personal integrity

What we do is the external expression of who we are. A lot of things I mentioned in the previous section talk about work habits or ethics that would help us prevent problems and detect future issues. Forming good habits in ministry will remove many obstacles. It's when we become careless that problems come. And for the most part, carelessness and lack of organization happens within our personal lives, and then shows in our ministry.

I pride myself in being very efficient. But sometimes, it's just a façade for cutting corners. I may be able to fool some people, but I won't be able to fool all people. And most of all, God knows. We must do things for God and not for man (Colossians 3:23). Knowing that God is with me and practicing the presence of God in my life helps me in doing my best. I can't help but think of the song from the *Police*: "Every step you take, every move you make . . . I'll be watching you."

Beyond habits, how we address sin plays a huge role in personal integrity—things we do, things we watch, and things that cause others to sin. For the most part, we hide sin pretty well. What we can't hide, though, is if we are indifferent when sin occurs. We may become numb to sin when we are around it too often, and it shows when our students see how we respond to certain situations. Examples of this would be our reaction to vulgar language, laughing at funny things that may be sacrilegious, or not realizing bad influences in our lives and in the lives of students.

For me, language is my weakness. I used to use bad language like crazy! But because of the movies I watched and because of some of my friends, I didn't notice bad language sometimes. Some parents saw this as me condoning students using bad language.

That is why it's important for us to lead with other people around us. People who can compensate for our weakness and who can make us aware of things we don't see that may be harmful. Accountability partners who can ask tough questions are extremely important. People who are close to us and can help us pinpoint our downfalls and shortcomings. It could be your wife who helps you, a prayer partner, an accountability partner, or members on your staff. Whoever it is, integrity starts in the private dimensions of our lives.

nobody's perfect

We will run into ruts in our ministry. Sometimes it's due to paradigm differences. Other times, it really is because of our mistakes and stupidity. When you're going 100 mph in a 65 mph zone, it's just lame to argue with the police officer. Especially when he has you clocked on his radar. The same thing goes for us in ministry. Arguing won't help. Accept it and admit fault when you really are at fault. Hiding doesn't help anyone. Running away will just make things worse. Take the hit. Face the music and hope that things will work out. As church leaders, we need to keep the peace at all costs (Ephesians 4:2-3). And out of all people, we are to be the examples for keeping peace, showing love, and displaying meekness.

wrapping it up

I got rid of my radar detector. I told my students that I had come to realize that even though owning a radar detector wasn't illegal, it put my character in question. And even though it helped me not to speed, it still raised questions as to why I own it. Things turned out good. I used my example as a lesson to the students, and all of us adjusted our lives in some way or fashion.

As for the story about the outraged parent, the family has not re-turned to the church. I now have to live with the fact that my actions drove this family away. Even though it was one flaw among many good things that are going on in the youth ministry, I have to live with the fact that this family was driven away from this church due to my carelessness and insensitivity.

Having something bad turned good is great. But then there are things, like with this outraged parent, where it didn't turn out too well. I lost sleep and spent a lot of time soul searching and praying. At times, I questioned if I was fit to do youth ministry. Was this something that was telling me about a deeper sin that was in my life that I avoided? Or was it just a little "oops" that was misunderstood?

Friends, realize this: as much as you try, your radars will not be able to prevent every snag that comes your way. Just as a radar detector does-n't guarantee you not getting a ticket, so it is with our radar detector in ministry. But just because you got a moving violation doesn't mean you stop driving. You pay off the ticket, go to traffic school, and then you get back out there and drive again. The same goes with us in ministry. We will be accused of things we didn't do and accused of things we did do. Accept it. Learn from it. And then get right back out there and be more careful next time, making sure that you have God's wisdom and discern-ment as you get back on the road of ministry.

lemonade lessons

1. Is there anything I'm doing that might bring the youth ministry in question? What is it? How can I eliminate it?

2. Is there anything the ministry team is doing that may bring the youth ministry in question? What is it? How can we eliminate it?

3. Are there any flaws in my own life that are unchecked right now?

4. Do I have people in my life who can honestly speak into my life and confront me on issues that might be hurtful to my ministry and life? Who are they? How effective have they been? How welcoming am I to their constructive criticism?

Joel Lusz

Joel was born in Spartanburg, South Carolina, to amazing Christian parents. As a high school student, Joel began to hear the call of God to go into full-time ministry. Joel attended Taylor University (where he played college basketball) and then graduated from Trinity Evangelical Divinity School in Deerfield, Illinois, with a Masters Degree in Counseling Psychology. In addition, Joel has been trained and educated by Jim Burns through his HomeWord ministries and is one of their speaker/trainers.

Joel's passion is in ministering to youth and families. He has been in ministry now for 25 years and continues to do speaking and training in the areas of Leadership Development, Multimedia In Ministry, Healthy Family/Parent Seminars, Training Youth Ministers and more. He is the co-author of several books, magazines, and articles.

Joel is married to his true love, Angie, and they have two beautiful daughters, Koral and Willow. Joel is Youth Pastor at Suntree United Methodist Church in Melbourne, Florida, where he continues his love for fishing, boating, beach volleyball, and following the Green Bay Packers. Joel co-founded an online ministry entitled GoYouthMinistry.com. GoYouthMinistry's desire is to support other youth ministries. Their motto is: "Here to help!"

To contact Joel:
Joeljoel@cfl.rr.com

lemon 9

from aliens to allies

(partnering with parents)

When I was a boy of fourteen, my father was so ignorant I could hardly stand to have the old man around. But when I got to be twenty-one, I was astonished by how much he'd learned in seven years.

—Mark Twain

from aliens . . .

I ran into Mrs. Carroll, a middle school student's mother, about ten minutes after our Wednesday night youth program had already started. We were upstairs in the lobby just outside of my office. I had forgotten something and was on my way to retrieve it. "What are you doing?" she asked. I told her I was on my way to my office to get some supplies for the night. "What are you doing?" I replied. "I'm on my way downstairs to observe you."

I thought, "Observe *me?*" Now that was unusual.

A few minutes later I was downstairs with a room full of kids, a handful of adult and college staff, and Mrs. Carroll . . . observing me. I knew right then and there: I hate parents!

> I was intimidated and, quite frankly, scared.

Things did not go well that night either! My timing was off. My jokes were not funny. And my lesson stunk. I was intimidated and, quite frankly, scared. I just knew that if I did not do a great job (and satisfy Mrs. Carroll completely) there would be a letter written to my boss, the Senior Pastor.

And sure enough, that's exactly what happened. And, of course, she copied it to me. It wasn't pretty. It detailed all the things I had done wrong and why I was unfit to be a youth director. Surely, I thought, she represents all parents!

I wish I could tell you that was an isolated experience. Unfortunately, that would not be true. In my 25 years of youth ministry, I've had more experiences like that than I care to remember. In fact, I started thinking about all of the challenges and confrontations I've had over the years, and I thought it would be fun to recount them here. Hopefully, my wallowing through these depressing episodes now will serve as an encouragement for you later!

> You won't read this in the Bible, but Jesus says we should not ...

My first encounter came at the hands of an irate father who literally walked through the front door of my house without knocking or asking! I lived in a church–owned residence, so I guess he figured it was okay! My home was a little messy (I was single and had two friends over to play some basketball), and he really lit into me. I was shocked! And after a good tongue–lashing, he did the craziest thing! He quoted Jesus by first saying: "You won't read this in the Bible, but Jesus says we should not have a messy house." I was so angry and yet, on the verge of laughter! I had just graduated from seminary and was pretty sure you're not supposed to quote Jesus if there's no written support (i.e. the Bible!) for what you're quoting.

Another time, I had a parent outline several "shortcomings" in my abilities as a youth director, and then he sent the outline, along with a letter, to the Senior Pastor and the church Session. He had a list of 21 points where I was falling short as the steward of the house I was living in! One accusation stated, "Some of the bricks around the garden are cracked. I don't think Joel understands his responsibility in living in and maintaining this house!" I was floored! I was single and lived in a house that had a volleyball court, a swimming pool, a barbeque pit, and a cool, wide–open porch—all of which were used for a huge teen hangout. In addition, we had cookouts, parties, our entire middle school and high school ministries there, and more! Of course it wasn't perfectly maintained. This guy, for some reason, had it against me!

These three stories represent numerous others that are untold. I battled parents for years, and it seemed like I was always on the losing end. Some of those battles seem very trivial now. But I believe each one, whether big or small, did damage to my ministry and ultimately to the kids I was called to help.

to allies . . .

But I think the final straw came when I realized after about ten years of ministry that I had no real, good adult/parent friends and little, if any, support from them. I began to understand how I had been undermining and sabotaging my own ministry by ostracizing parents and their part in the youth program. It was as if the proverbial light finally came on! It hit me: Parents can *make* a youth ministry, or they can *break* a youth ministry. And for the most part, the direction that ends up taking is up to me. So, shortly after this revelation, I started a ministry with and to

> Parents can *make* a youth ministry, or they can *break* a youth ministry.

parents I called *Parents as Partners*. That shift in thinking and my new way of doing things has made all the difference in the world!

"Fake it until you make it." When I first heard that quote, I wasn't sure exactly what it meant. But as I began to think about my new approach to ministry (and to moms and dads), its subtle wisdom began to sink in. I knew that I needed to change me first—and that wasn't going to be easy! I had a strong bias against parents and for the most part, I figured they felt the same way toward me. So I knew right then and there that I needed to take a new, fresh, positive posture in my dealings with parents.

Here's where the change began:

First, my prayer life changed. Now, I'm not saying that I became super spiritual, but I did begin to commit some time to bringing this before the Lord. I figured not only did I need his guidance and power, but I also figured God's a daddy who's probably very eager to help me!

Second, I purposely looked at parents differently. I imaged that they were probably as eager as I was to grow their kids as young followers of Christ. I saw them as peers and as friends who had the same interests that I had! They loved their kid, struggled in some areas with them, and prayed for them when alone. Parents were not the enemy after all. The real enemy was my thinking—and that was changing!

> I figured not only did I need his guidance and power, but I also figured God's a daddy who's probably very eager to help me.

Third, I began an intensive recruiting campaign to get parents on my team. I began to realize that I didn't need a bunch of longhaired, surfer dudes who played guitar and drove a mini-van to be the only volunteers doing youth ministry. Sure, I'd take a handful of Christians like that any day, but I knew we also needed caring, Christian adults. I foolishly believed that only younger college-type students instinctively knew how to minister to young people. I was way wrong! Once I made that shift in my thinking, and once I began to build a balanced team of both young and old (particularly parents), the ministry I oversaw began to mature and become much healthier.

to partnering with parents . . .

I live along the east coast of Florida where the sun is hot, the beach is "cool," and the fishing is about the best in the world. So, not too long ago, I bought a boat for my family. And now one of our favorite hobbies is to go out into the intra-coastal waterway or the Atlantic Ocean for a day on the water. Navigating the calm seas of the nearest river usually isn't too tough. But imagine a larger boat with a crew of about 15 or so teenagers who, for the most part, have no idea how to guide a water vessel. Who steers? What is the best way to cut through a wave? How do you "read" the channel markers? Without the guidance of an experienced shipman, that boat could be in serious trouble! Now picture the same

A potentially dangerous journey now becomes a pleasure ride with purpose!

boat with the same crew and a handful of adults (working along *with* the teens) who are sea savvy. A potentially dangerous journey now becomes a pleasure ride with purpose! The same is true in youth ministry when parents are "on board!"

A youth director who makes parents and families a top priority has gone a long way to insuring that his or her youth ministry is successful. Parents can become (and should become) your greatest support and your biggest cheerleaders. They have the ability to put out many "small fires" and ultimately can become a rock upon which to build your ministry.

the definite dozen

Since "coming of age" and getting tired of "banging my head against the same rock," I have come up with what I call my "Definite Dozen" to help in the dream of partnering with the parents of the kids in my ministry. I believe they are nearly "non-negotiable" and should provide a definite impact to the health and life of any youth program.

1. Communicate, communicate, communicate! You cannot over-communicate to the parents of your students all that is happening in your ministry. Go overboard! We use cell phones, a Sunday morning Newsletter (*each* and *every* Sunday!), email, announcements, flyers, posters, a parent's bulletin board, and more! I believe the number one frustration among parents is this: *They don't know what's going on!* Communicating with them creates a sense of comfort, trust, and a feeling of dependability and maturity. It is probably the single most important thing we can do to partner with parents!

2. Use their first names. I don't care how young you are or how old they are. Addressing parents by name puts you in the same category with them—adulthood. They will see you as a peer and someone to be respected, not as an immature kid.

> I believe the number one frustration among parents is this: They don't know what's going on!

3.   Write   them   letters. Nothing encourages, pleases, and lifts-up a parent like a positive letter from an adult who loves and cares for their child. Paul tells us in 1 Thessalonians 5:11: "Therefore encourage one another and build each other up, just as in fact you are doing." Parents usually receive only bad news from adults regarding their child. So an encouraging note goes a long, long way. You'll not only build a rapport with that parent, you'll also grow your relationship with his child. And guess what? It's your job! So be an encourager by writing encouraging letters.

4.   Be a "Parent Cheerleader." Look for opportunities to speak highly of the parents in your ministry. Build them up verbally in their presence and in their absence. You'll soon earn a reputation as someone who likes, respects, and enjoys the parents around you.

5.   Recruit them as youth ministry volunteers. I think we live by a myth in youth ministry, and the myth is this: Parents don't want to be around their kid, and their kid doesn't want the parents around. I think that's absurd! Now I know in some instances and with some parent/child relationships, this is true (and that is sad!). But for the most part, I think the two truly want to be together. You have to respect space and personal issues, but my best volunteers are almost always moms and dads!

6.   Do not speak poorly about the parents of the kids in your group. I always try to communicate with kids that I'm on their parent's side! (I also tell them that I'm on *their* side as well!) When you make jokes about parents, undermine their responsibility or parenting style, or insult them, you do a lot of damage—to *their* family and *your* ministry.

7.   Use your "Asker." What is that you ask? We are so often intimidated by parents that we tend to shy away from interacting with them. If the truth is known, parents are actually eager to lend a helping hand. Be courageous and bold enough to ask! All they can do is say "no" (which rarely happens). But if they say "yes," you've not only begun a new relationship with a parent, but you've begun building your team! Ask parents! Ask them for help. Ask them for advice. Ask them to head things up. You'll be amazed at the good that comes from it!

8. Tell parents you love them! That sounds crazy, doesn't it? Try it. Here's what I mean: Whenever you have a get-together with parents, let them know how much you appreciate them, want them involved in your ministry, and love them! It can sometimes sound funny, but "there is truth in jest!" John tells us in 1 John 4:7 "Dear friends, let us love one another, for love comes from God. Everyone who loves has been born of God and knows God." They will leave knowing that you're on their side, and you truly want their participation in what you're overseeing.

9. Develop a Parents Ministry. I know you're busy and have plenty to do. So you'll have to be strategic about this one. Here's what we do: First, we kick off each "season" with a parent's night. We do not change anything, we just invite the parents to join us and then continue with our regular program. Second, we do an occasional event with parents (softball game, dinner and a movie, etc.). And finally, we try to have a once-per-year large event like a seminar or parenting workshop. And usually, we have a parent head that up!

> Do not speak poorly about the parents of the kids in your group.

10. Take them to lunch. Or dinner. Or breakfast. Get out of the office and develop a relationship with them! Let them see your heart and passion for ministry and for their child. And by the way, pay the bill!

11. Be a friend. This point truly falls under the category of "strategic planning!" Look at those moms and dads and see how plausible it is for you to take your relationship beyond the youth group walls to the outside world. Hang out with them. Play golf with them. Take them on your boat (one of my favorites!). By developing a friendship that will grow over the weeks, months, and years, your ministry will no longer be "shallow," but deep.

12. Pray with and for your parents. It's nearly impossible to dislike one another and not grow together when you're in prayer together. Inviting God and parents into your ministry plan can only bring about great results! When you reach out and hold the hand of a parent and bow your head in prayer, you're truly doing ministry and not merely just programming.

13. Be the church! The beginning of the church, as written about in Acts 2:42 reads, "They devoted themselves to the apostles' teaching and to the fellowship, to the breaking of bread and to prayer." We sometimes get into the thinking that parents and other adults are here to serve us and help our little dynasties. In reality, we're here to serve them and help build the community of God, the body of Christ. When we realize that, that will change our approach to ministry and how we relate to parents.

> Develop a friendship that will grow over the weeks, months and years and your ministry will no longer be "shallow," but deep.

Those are my "Definite Dozen" (plus a bonus!), and if you'll consider applying them to the ministry you oversee, you'll definitely see amazing results. The "battle" with parents does not need to be a reality. If you'll change your thinking and your approach, you'll realize before too long that parents can become your allies, instead of aliens, as you learn to partner together for God!

lemonade lessons

1. What is the worst youth ministry experience you've ever had with a parent?

2. What is your mindset when it comes to the parents of the students in your youth program?

3. Why do you think parents are more often seen as aliens and not as allies?

4. Do you agree that parents can make or break a youth program? Explain.

5. Which of the "Definite Dozen" resonated most with you and why?

6. Discuss the "boat" analogy and what it means for your current youth program.

7. What's your plan now?

Matt Genos

Matt has been involved with student ministries for ten years. He has a passion to lead students and volunteers in the ways of Jesus. One of his growing interests is to come alongside ministry leaders and volunteers in order to equip them through consultation, coaching, and training. If you don't find Matt scheming to locate Buckeye tickets, you will find him doing something active outdoors or traveling with his wife Jenny and their three sons, Riley, Ethan, and Jacob. They live in Toledo, Ohio, where Matt is Pastor of Junior High Ministry at Westgate Chapel.

To contact Matt:
mgenos@westgatechapel.org

when your circle of trust implodes

(know who, when, and how to trust others)

Do not trust all men, but trust men of worth;
the former course is silly, the latter a mark of prudence.[13]

—Democritus

Many of the stories that are shared in this book revolve around one key element of ministry leadership . . . TRUST. Why is trust so important? All student ministries involve people, and the leading of people requires trust. (Just ask Moses!) As we thumb back through the failures represented here, you'll soon realize that many of us miscalculated, abused, or disregarded trust in some way. The tearing down of trust manifests itself in many different ways and is the result of varying reasons. But the results are amazingly similar. Lack of trust gives birth to broken relationships, criticism, suspicion, lack of support, and ultimately strips the leader of the ability to influence. This lack of influence can involve one student, a family, or it can spread to encompass the entire ministry.

The most difficult thing about trust is that it's like a delicate flower.

> As with many things in life, we're awakened through a moment of complete failure.

When it's given proper care, it flourishes and brings light, color, and life to a room and its occupants. But when it's left to itself or handled too often, it withers and dies. Just like a flower, proper care doesn't involve one single step. Proper trust is the result of a web of many interrelated items. Unfortunately, many of us become aware of this through hindsight. As with many things in life, we're awakened through a moment of complete failure. For some reason, we take trust for granted until it is withered and dead.

Obviously, the leadership failure I want to share with you, like many others, involves trust that withered and died. The twist with my story is that it was my trust that was broken—not the other way around. On the surface, this might invoke a greater amount of sympathy. But the result of blindly placing trust in other leaders often leads to greater consequences. My hope is that you can learn from my experience and avoid a withered and dead trust.

Early in my first ministry, exciting things were beginning to happen. I was Pastor of Youth in a small, rural town in northern Wisconsin, where everyone knew one another, and students were always "hanging around." There weren't a lot of options for students. No other church had a passion to connect with them. Like many subcultures, these students came from broken homes and experienced one dysfunctional relationship after another. Our church had a vision to use their location to engage students and see them connect with Jesus and his message of hope. Students of all types entered our ministry community looking for love, relationships, healing, and hope. My wife and I still remember these days with a special fondness because the students we were reaching were unchurched, unloved, and looking for something bigger than themselves. With the overwhelming support of the entire congregation, it did not take long before our group of 20 or so students began to grow. This rapid growth was a huge blessing and reverberated throughout the church. But it put strains on our volunteer staff's ability to properly minister to these students. This strain set the stage for my leadership fiasco.

When my wife, Jenny, and I arrived, we had a team of four leaders, including us, to direct the ministry. This team quickly dwindled to three. (My awesome leadership abilities accounts for this negative growth.) So here we were with a group of students that had tripled in size, and an adult-to-student ratio approaching 20-to-1. We had lots of issues ranging from improper room size to inappropriate behavior when meeting as a group. I had (and still have) a passion to become a group of small groups. Looking out over this hungry group, God made it plain to me that the only way to meet their needs and connect them with the ways of Jesus was to ensure that they had a shepherd to care for them and lead them on an intimate and personal level. The other important element that God made clear was that I must work hard at assembling a team that would embrace and embody this vision. This became my driving passion. Locating people to shepherd students consumed my every move. I couldn't rest until this need was met.

Locating willing individuals was a daunting task. Locating individuals with a foundational skill set was darn near impossible. As I began to talk with individuals, God raised up a few people who were willing and ready to learn. Our team began to grow. Fortunately, these people were well grounded and willing to learn on the fly. Our need to diversify was great because our group of students quickly approached triple figures.

> Locating people to shepherd students consumed my every move. I couldn't rest until this need was met.

During this time, Jenny and I began to build relationships with two individuals, Jack and Sara*. Jack, like many men in our congregation, came from a nominal church background. The thought of serving in a relational setting had never crossed his mind. Men in our church weren't anti-relational. Relational serving simply never registered on their radar. Men in the town and church were hard workers, but only behind the scenes. Women dominated serving roles within the church. Nevertheless,

Jack had a hunger to grow, so I jumped on the opportunity, knowing that willing men were an endangered species. I quickly placed Jack as a shepherd over a group of boys and challenged him to have faith and learn as he led.

During this same period, Jenny was introduced to Sara. Jenny was in the middle school almost every day as a substitute teacher, and Sara taught Spanish in the school district. Sara was an enigma. In a town were people rarely experienced things outside their county and state, Sara stood out as a world traveler. She was well-versed in different cultures, religions, and literature. These are the things that drew Jenny to her almost instantly. During one of their initial conversations (after finding out Jenny was a Christ-follower), Sara shared a powerful insight. She said, "I have read religious literature from all of the other religions. But when I read the Bible, I knew it was true." Sara had lived abroad, married someone from another country, experienced a bitter divorce, and found herself hurting and lonely. The truth she found in Scripture led her to Christ. She instantly began to look for a church. Because of her friendship with Jenny, she started attending our church. The change in Sara was monumental and, like Jack, she had a hunger to grow. Noticing her obvious love for students, we asked her to join our volunteer staff and lead a group of girls. She eagerly accepted. My trust in both of them was immediate.

> Jack and Sara were student magnets. I had hit a gold mine!

Jack and Sara were student magnets. I had hit a gold mine! Sara had an amazing ability to attract girls who were wounded and bitter. They latched on to her and came face to face with Christ. Jack's calm, laid back presence quickly created trust between him and his guys. During this time, Jack and Sara also joined a small group with Jenny and me. Things were going well, and I was satisfied because a critical piece of the vision was beginning to take shape.

As our year moved into the winter, Jack and Sara had a growing interest in each other. Jenny and I, as did others, looked positively on this. They seemed to "spur each other on to love and good deeds" (Hebrews 10:24). Their relationship quickly became the "darling" of our ministry.

They seemed to handle themselves in a righteous manner, and we trusted them without question. As their relationship progressed, Jack and Sara got engaged and began to plan their life together. They purchased a home together, and Sara took occupancy eagerly awaiting their wedding day. As wedding plans progressed, people began to notice a change in their passions and demeanor. After being the catalyst for our small group, they began to find any excuse available to avoid meeting with us. Many of the other members of our group began to have severe reservations about their relationship. Students (especially leadership students) began to murmur about certain things that created questions in their minds. They would see Jack's car at the house (the house was on the same road as the high school) for what seemed to be long periods of time—maybe overnight. They were struggling with what seemed to be a contradiction between what they said and what they did. As these questions arose, Jack and Sara seemed to pull themselves away from relationships that would sharpen them. Instead, they turned toward relationships that would affirm their every move.

At this juncture, it would be appropriate to ask, "What was I doing during this intensifying storm?" I continued to support Jack and Sara by blindly trusting them as I had from the beginning. In hindsight, this seems like a horrible decision (and was), but during this time I had other forces driving my decisions. First, I'm a very trusting person. I assume the best—suspicion is not something that easily enters my frame of reference. Second, I was thinking about the need for good leaders. (Remember, this was my overriding passion.) Jack and Sara were phenomenal leaders . . . minus their current moral situation. Students loved them. If I did what was necessary, we would lose certain students who only related to Jack and Sara. In the back of my mind, I was thinking about what we would do with their small groups. Third, the end of the year was nearing, and if our suspicions were true, I would deal with them after the school year was done. This would allow me to release Jack and Sara without a big scene among the students. In the end, I simply was *trusting* that this would all go away. My ability as a leader to judge character was on the line. My trust had been broken, and I didn't want to deal with it. I continued down the path of blind trust to the bitter end.

> In the end, I had to deal with all the same issues; they were simply bigger in scope and harder to explain. Trust had withered and died.

Ultimately, this story has no happy ending. My course of action allowed Jack and Sara's choices to go unchecked. The guilt of their choices, in addition to my lack of confrontation, drove them away from God and the church. They split up, went their own ways, and returned to their former lives. They both still live in the community, but might as well be in another universe. I have not spoken to either one of them in over six years. Ironically, all the reasons I used to maintain blind trust and avoid confrontation became reality. For instance, some of the students who connected with them had an impossible time reconciling all the facts, so these students also returned to their previous lives. In the end, I had to deal with all the same issues; they were simply bigger in scope and harder to explain. Trust had withered and died.

I long for these wounds to find some sort of healing for all parties involved. Until that time arrives, I find some comfort in offering some lessons I learned from this leadership fiasco. I hope that these foundational elements of trust will enable you to build a trusted web of volunteers and avoid trust that withers and dies.

never let NEED drive your TRUST

It is easy for us as youth workers to get overwhelmed by the needs of our students. In our current culture, students are experiencing brokenness, pain, and abandonment at an earlier age and in an intensifying manner. Any youth worker worth her salt is holistically affected by the students under her care. But we have to be honest and remember the words of Jesus, "The harvest is plentiful, but the workers are few" (Matthew 9:37). We will never form a team that can adequately meet every need represented by our students. Don't take this as a discouraging word. If our **NEEDS** drive everything else, we will make poor decisions about **TRUST**. We will place people in positions to fill needs without adequate time to build an appropriate trust level. This was my overriding mistake. It is better to take the time needed to build trust so that ministry can take place over the long haul instead of meeting needs in the short run. We can look to Jesus for this model. Instead of trying to meet every immediate need, he invested in a few people and built mutual trust so that future generations would be affected. The former sets us on a path for hope, while the latter sets us up for discouragement and failure.

don't let broken trust turn you into a skeptic

Once trust is broken and shattered, it's easy for a leader to stay at arms-length distance. This seems like the easiest way to avoid disaster. This is a self-defense mechanism that's meant to protect you from future painful experiences. It's true that this reaction will protect you from pain, but it will also prevent you from experiencing love and joy. In order to experience God's greatest for us, our leadership, and the people we are leading, we have to be willing to allow for the possibility of experiencing the greatest pain. These two things are directly proportionate. The level at which we can experience love is directly related to the level in which we are willing to experience pain. Trust, properly placed, will never remove the possibility of pain. It simply opens up doors for us to experience the greatest love. All healthy ministries are based on relationships. True relationships can never form if we approach them as a skeptic due to past pain. We need to learn from our pain—not avoid it.

> . . . what loneliness is more lonely than distrust?[14]
>
> – George Eliot
> author

trust is a team contact sport

As leaders we need to take the approach of Paul when it comes to building proper trust among volunteers. Paul says in 1 Thessalonians 2:8, "We loved you so much that we were delighted to share with you not only

> The only way to make a man trustworthy is to trust him; and the surest way to make him untrustworthy is to distrust him and show your distrust.[15]
>
> – Henry L. Stinson
> U.S. politician

the gospel of God but our lives as well, because you had become so dear to us." In order to properly create trust, we must intentionally build a community among our volunteers. They must see that they are called to spiritual formation within a community—not just a ministry job. By inviting volunteers to a community driven by spiritual formation, an environment of mutual accountability, encouragement, and loving exhortation can begin. This can protect the ministry from a situation ballooning to the point of the one I shared. It acts as a change agent based on love for each other. It also places any needed confrontation within the realm of the team instead on the lap of the ministry leader. If volunteers do not experience this kind of community, they will see themselves as an island. This sets the stage for failure without loving, grace-giving confrontation and success without proper encouragement. In the end, a team environment not only strengthens trust and accountability, it also spills over into the lives of the students. *Whatever is a realized value of your team of volunteers will become a realized value for your students.*

trust is earned, not given

I know this is a cliché, but its simple truth is often overlooked. If we begin to see trust as a team contact sport, we must set up a system that encourages success instead of failure. We must create an attitude within the team where everyone acknowledges that trust, no matter who you are, is incremental. In order to do this, you, as the leader, need to invite people to mentored roles where individuals do not automatically assume sole leadership in any area of ministry. Allow them to enter as apprentices, regardless of their spiritual maturity and experience. This establishes protection for all involved parties right from the start. It allows volunteers to receive responsibility at the proper rate. Some volunteers will rise to leadership roles within months, while others may take years. I have experienced both, and I never had anyone refuse to volunteer because we did not anoint her with a specific role. And if someone does react like that, I believe it serves as proof that she is not ready to join the team. These levels of trust help create a sacrificial servant attitude within your team by placing the ministry and community above any single individual.

When we boil these foundational elements of trust down, we are faced with one overriding quality . . . TIME. I believe this is why we youth workers often ignore these elements until we come face to face with failure. Long-term anything is something with which we are unfamiliar. We look at the present and sense its urgency. The future is now! But we can't ignore the time it takes to develop the trust necessary to form a web volunteers. If we do, we will end up with a ministry that is withered and dead.

names have been changed

Personal Reflections:

1. Do you tend to trust too quickly or are you overly skeptical? How can you work towards a healthy balance?

2. Do you avoid building relationship with volunteers because of past pain?

3. What current areas/needs do you feel pressured to expand, develop, or meet? Do you place these above relationships with others? Do you trust God to meet the needs before you?

4. Are you so untrusting that you try to do everything yourself? What steps could you take to begin building a web of trusted volunteers?

Group Reflection

5. What would have happened if Jesus tried to meet every need immediately rather than taking the time to develop a team that could carry out ministry once Jesus returned to his Father?

6. What is the health level of our volunteer staff? Do we foster and environment of trust, encouragement, and loving confrontation?

7. What system of checks and balances do we have set up within our team? Are there any elements we could add to protect the ministry and each other?

8. Assuming we do have an appropriate system in place, how should confrontation and restoration be handled in the light of failure?

Kent Julian

Kent Julian is a veteran youth worker and well-traveled speaker who currently serves as the National Director of Alliance Youth (of the C&MA), an organization that works with more than 2,000 church youth ministries in the United States. Kent is also a regular contributor to various magazines, has authored several books, trains for several youth ministry organizations, and is the founder of Live It Forward™, a wildly successful business that helps the younger generation discover their life and career calling (you can find out about Live It Forward at www.liveitforward.com).

Okay, enough of the "promo" stuff. If you really want to know Kent, you need to know his favorite pastimes include hanging out with his incredible wife, Kathy, and their three awesome children, exercising, eating sushi, reading, and sipping Kenya coffee at Starbucks. He is totally comfortable with his baldness, and students and youth workers alike are inspired by Kent's humor, story telling, and passion.

To contact Kent:
info@liveitforward.com
770-339-8116

conclusion

mixing youth ministry lemonade

When fate hands you a lemon, make lemonade.

—Dale Carnegie

Youth ministry compilation books, like this one, are unique. They offer different insights from different youth workers leading different ministries. In addition, each author has a different writing style and different opinions. Yet even with all these differences, one message stands out: *youth ministry lemons, if processed correctly, can turn into youth ministry lemonade!*

So, as you wrap up this unique book filled with all its different insights and suggestions, I imagine you and I sitting at my second office—a favorite coffee shop of mine and the place where I most often meet people. We'd share our "sour" youth ministry stories and ask each other all kinds of questions. And if you were in the midst of a "sour" experience and wanted some advice, I would challenge you with two simple words:

START MIXING!

These two words encompass the secret of making youth ministry lemonade. They speak of embracing mistakes, learning from them, and taking steps to move on. Making youth ministry lemonade is really that simple.

I'd also share a few other thoughts I've come to call the *E's of Excellence* (I know, corny . . . but it helps me remember). These ideas can play a role in making your youth ministry "sweeter."

> I want to make lemonade out of the lemons that were dealt to me.[16]
>
> – Baron Hill
> U.S. Congressman

First, remember that truly successful youth ministries focus on the *environment* within their group. These ministries understand that God (not event, programs, or youth workers) transforms teenagers. Therefore, they focus on cultivating an environment within their group that is conducive to God doing his work when and how he wants. They pour all their energy into environmental issues and trust God for life-changing results.

Second, speaking of trusting God, "sweet" youth ministries create an air of *expectancy*. Do you believe God is "able to do immeasurably more than all we ask or imagine" (Ephesians 3:20)? Are you living and leading accordingly? In many ways, we get what we expect, so go ahead and live as if you really believe God can do more than you can imagine. As many of the authors of this book will testify, when you do, he does . . . even in the midst of "sour" experiences!

Third, as long as you are going to have an attitude of expectancy, be sure to also do your part and *exceed expectations.* Whether you agree with popular self-help guru Wayne Dyer or not, he is definitely right about one thing . . . "It's never crowded along the extra mile." So travel the extra mile and exceed expectations. I hate saying this, but youth ministry attracts many people who use being "relational" and "authentic" as excuses for laziness. By all means, be relational and authentic, but be that way while striving for excellence. In many instances, it is our lack of *excellence* (there's another "e" word) that creates "sour" experiences. So don't make excuses (and yet another "e" word). Instead, champion excellence.

Fourth, even though you should strive to excel, don't forget to embrace simplicity. Mixing lemonade is not complicated; it's simply taking all our experiences (both "sour" and "sweet"), mixing them up, and then learning and growing from them. Therefore, if you want to mix youth ministry lemonade, don't make things too hard. Focus on one or two lessons from this book and apply them to your life. Soon, you will likely experience a new kind of "sweetness" in your group.

Finally, *earnestly lean into* the opportunities God grants you. No matter if you are in the midst of a "sour" experience or "sweet" times, when you are available to God, he usually shows up and works through you. And God showing up—more than great resources, spectacular facilities, or dynamic programs—is what creates momentum.

I hope you have enjoyed reading this book as much as we have enjoyed writing it. Our prayer is that it won't be just another resource that is put on your shelf never to be looked at again, but is one that will inspire both volunteers and full-time youth workers to see their mistakes as opportunities for leadership successes. Remember, when we are weak, God is strong!

With great respect and admiration for who you are and what you do,
Kent Julian (for the entire writing team)

> I made stupid decisions as a kid, or as a young adult, but I'm trying to take this lemon and make lemonade.[17]
>
> – Kevin Mitnick
> famous criminal hacker

The Inside Out Youth Worker™
Discovering the ArtWork of Making Disciples

A new book that offers a biblical, holistic approach for youth workers!

From the back cover:

You don't have to be ultra hip, off-the-hook, or super cool to be a great youth worker, but you do need to be inside out. Not backwards. . . **just inside out.**

What does it mean to be inside out? It's learning to follow Jesus in such a way that he not only lives in you, he impacts teenagers through you. It's allowing your "doing" to flow from your "being."

From start to finish, *The Inside Out Youth Worker*™ is about making disciples of Jesus Christ among teenagers. Yet, unlike many youth ministry books about disciple-making, this one doesn't focus on programs, processes, systems, or structures. It's all about you—the youth worker. For the authors of this book, the starting point for any discussion about making disciples in youth ministry is with youth workers themselves—who they are and what they should be about.

Getting it right here is 80% of the battle. Miss this and the most strategic programs matter very little. Being inside out is that important!

Here's what others are saying about the book:

"I love this approach to thinking about youth ministry!"
—Mark Oestreicher, President, Youth Specialties

"*The Inside Out Youth Worker*™ has its heart in exactly the right place—namely, that the best youth ministry 'strategy' is the power of a transformed

life. This book is both practical and challenging, and will not only upend the way you see ministry, but might just change your life."
—Rick Lawrence, Executive Editor, Group Magazine

"This practical and insightful book will undoubtedly help youth workers, the veteran and new recruit alike, more fully realize what it means to develop followers of Jesus—from the inside out."
—Chris Folmsbee, President, Sonlife Ministries

"Kent Julian and his very experienced youth ministry specialists have done an outstanding job helping us understand the 'being' art and 'doing' work of making disciples."
—Jim Burns, PhD, President, HomeWord

ISBN: 09777363-0-X

To order *The Inside Out Youth Workers*, visit:
www.insideoutyouthworker.com

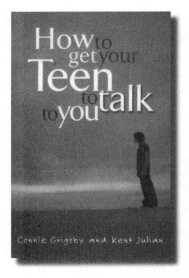

Connie Grigsby and Kent Julian

WANT TO BREAK THROUGH THE COMMUNICATION ROAD-BLOCKS WITH YOUR TEEN?

What turns your teen off and on in terms of communication? Do you find yourself talking with him or *at* him? What will it take to open her heart—or his mouth, for that matter?

If you love your teen but find the communication lines jumbled lately, the ideas in this book will help! Research constantly reveals: If you're a parent, you ARE the most important person in your teenager's life. And with a little help in the translation, you may find out she's been telling you that all along.

Definitely one of the best books I've ever read on communicating with teenagers.
—Wayne Rice, Co-founder of Youth Specialties

This book offers a straightforward approach to building communication skills with your teenager. It addresses one of the most challenging areas of parenting teens with simple, easy-to-follow language and ideas that will help you create an environment where communication happens naturally in your home.
—Doug Fields, High School Pastor, Saddleback Church

Kent and Connie give you all the tools you need to build the communication bridge.
—Barry St. Clair, President, Reach Out Youth Solutions

This book has fifty-two incredibly practical lessons on how to develop a better relationship with your teenager. It is practical, challenging, and affirming—a must-read for every parent!
—Jim Burns, PhD, President, HomeWord

ISBN: 1-59052-064-5

To order *How To Get Your Teen To Talk To You,* visit:
www.liveitforward.com

Notes

1. Robert T. Kiyosaki with Sharon L. Lechter, *Before You Quit Your Job* (New York: Warner Book Group, 2005), 37.
2. Taken from: http://www.brainyquote.com/quotes/authors/f/ freddie_mercury.html
3. M. Craig Barnes, *Sacred Thirst* (Grand Rapids: Zondervan, 2001), 187.
4. Erwin McManus, *Uprising* (Nashville: Thomas Nelson, 2003), 253.
5. Oswald Chambers, *My Utmost for His Highest* (Grand Rapids: Discovery House Publishers, 1992), October 3 devotion.
6. Wayne Martindale and Jerry Root, *The Quotable Lewis* (Carol Streams: Tyndale Publishers, 1990), 468.
7. Chambers, Ibid.
8. Taken from: http://www.retirementwithapurpose.com/quotes/ quotesprayer.html
9. Jim Burns and Greg McKinnon, *Illustrations, Stories, and Quotes to Hang Your Message On* (Ventura: Gospel Light, 1997), 210.
10. Taken from: The Quotation Page website: http://www.quotation-spage.com/quote/23218.html
11. Leonard Sweet, *Out of the Question . . . Into the Mystery* (Colorado. Springs: Waterbrook Press, 2004), 93.
12. Dean Merrill, *Vol. 3: Clergy Couples in Crisis : The Impact of Stress*

on Pastoral Marriages (Carol Stream, IL: The Leadership Library, 1985), 67.

13. Taken from: http://www.crypto.ch/

14. Taken from: http://www.worldofquotes.com/topic/Distrust/index.html

15. Taken from: http://www.randomhouse.com/catalog/display.pperl/display.pperl?isbn=9781578568017&view=printexcerpt

16. Taken from: http://www.brainyquote.com/quotes/quotes/b/baronhill203627.html

17. Taken from: http://www.brainyquote.com/quotes/quotes/k/kevinmitni234020.html